BREATHING

BREATHING

ON YOUR OWN

QUOTATIONS FOR INDEPENDENT THINKERS

RICHARD KEHL

DARLING & COMPANY

TABLE OF CONTENTS

TABLE OF CONTENTS

ISBN 1-883211-41-7

FIRST PRINTING ALL RIGHTS RESERVED
PRINTED IN SINGAPORE

DARLING & COMPANY
POST OFFICE BOX 31969 SEATTLE WASHINGTON 98103

BREATHING

ADVENTURE

Each moment is a place you've never been.

MARK STRAND

Beyond the wild wood comes the wide world, said the rat. And that's something that doesn't matter either to you or me. I've never been there, and I'm never going, nor you either, if you've got any sense at all. Don't ever refer to it again, please.

KENNETH GRAHAME

No mistake's made once: that's an adventure.

DAVID MUS

There are a number of very important irreversibles to be discovered in our universe. One of them is that every time you make an experiment you learn more: quite literally, you can not learn less.

BUCKMINSTER FULLER

Like the Zen poet followed by a servant carrying his liquor supply for the day and a spade, the spade to be used to dig a grave in case the master doesn't survive his next adventure.

And the end of all our exploring will be to arrive where we started and know the place for the first time.

T.S. ELIOT

...as the arrow endures the string, and in the gathering momentum becomes more than itself. Because to stay is to be nowhere.

RAINER MARIA RILKE

If you're doing anything you know you can do, you're not doing anything.

W.D. SNODGRASS

AMBIGUITY

Robert Graves once said that the supreme gift bestowed on the poet by the Muse was that of poetic humor, and that in its final draft a poem would become so perfectly ambivalent as to make him wonder whether the insertion of a simple "not" wouldn't perhaps improve it.

THE LONDON SUNDAY TIMES

When it comes to nuclear weapons you have to be very clear that you are being ambiguous.

GOVERNMENT SPOKESMAN FOR MARGARET THATCHER

Ambiguous facts have always a great fascination for me, for they seem to me to be located at just those intersections where the real nature of things may be revealed.

JEAN DUBUFFET

...the terrible ambiguity of immediate experience.

CARL JUNG

David Bohm argues that ambivalence is a fundamental but generally unrecognized aspect of creative thought. "Any particular thought" Bohm says, "will arouse the notion of its opposite by simply adding 'not'."

The creator's ability to tolerate ambivalence may be what poet John Keats called a "Negative Capability," that is, when a person "is capable of being in uncertainties, mysteries, doubts, without any irritable reaching after fact and reason."

JOHN BRIGGS

ART

As the lady said, "Well, if it isn't art, then I like it."

JOHN CAGE

There are chemists who spend their whole lives trying to find out what's in a lump of sugar. I want to know one thing. What is color?

PABLO PICASSO

I decided to start anew - to strip away what I had been taught, to accept as true my own thinking. This was one of the best times of my life. I was alone and singularly free working on my own, unknown – no one to satisfy but myself. I began with charcoal and paper and decided not to use any color until it was impossible to do what I wanted to do in black and white. I believe it was June before I needed blue.

GEORGIA O'KEEFFE

Art to me was a state; it didn't need to be an accomplishment.

MARGARET ANDERSON

In his final days, Max Ernst wrote self-effacingly that he wished to be remembered simply, in the words of the poet Rene Crevel, as "a magician of barely detectable displacements."

To draw a living line and not tremble from knowing it to be in danger of death at every point along its way, I must sleep in a sort of slumber allowing the sources of my life to flow without restraint into my hand, so that my hand ends by working alone, by flying into a dream, by moving without any care for me.

JEAN COCTEAU

When my daughter was about seven years old, she asked me one day what I did at work. I told her I worked at the college – that my job was to teach people how to draw. She stared back at me, incredulous, and said, "You mean they forget?"

HOWARD IKEMOTO

What strip mining is to nature, the art market has become to culture.

ROBERT HUGHES

The Zen master calligrapher Hakuin (1687-1769) when asked how long it took him to produce a single work rendered in simple bold strokes, replied, "Ten seconds and 80 years."

Duchamp never worked on his art for more than two hours a day, when he was working on it at all. Part of his work on "Large Glass" involved letting it gather dust for six months.

I have worked for years just to have people say, "So that's all Matisse is."

HENRI MATISSE

Alain Le Foll never considered illustration or commercial work inferior to the "fine" arts. He was convinced that there is no minor form of artistic expression and that an artist reveals himself completely at all times, in everything he does.

On a recent visit to the Metropolitan Museum of Art, I was standing near two women who were admiring a painting. One of the women remarked: "What a beautiful painting. I wonder who the artist was?" The other volunteered to find out and walked over to read the wall plaque beside it. She reported that the painting had been done by Circa, in 1878. "Oh," the first woman said, "of course, Circa the Greek." "No," the second woman replied. "You're thinking of Zorba. Circa was Italian."

KENNETH R. LEE

Surely, all art is the result of one's having been in danger, of having gone through an experience all the way to the end, where no one can go any further.

RAINER MARIA RILKE

Dubuffet has proposed a museum of banal skills. (such as blowing smoke rings)

BREATHING ON YOUR OWN

If the artist has total freedom — if art can be anything the artist says it is — it will also never be anything more than that.

PETER FULLER

I once knew a crazy woman who worked with her hands in the air. She made sculptures in the air. I didn't think she was doing anything. But, since she was crazy, she used flour for makeup. She was always making immobile sculptures in the air. But one day she moved her face and the flour fell from her face like a cloud covering up something in the air. And I saw a beautiful geometrical form. Then I took a bag of flour, went into her room and started to throw the flour around in the air. And beautiful sculptures began to appear. That's the story.

ALEXANDRO JODOROWSKY

I can assure you, that once you get rid of the notion of art, you acquire a great many wonderful new freedoms.

JEAN TINGUELY

Art is science in the flesh.

JEAN COCTEAU

I read somewhere that Rubens said students should not draw from life, but draw from all the great classic casts. Then you really get the measure of them, you really know what to do. And then, put in your own dimples. Isn't that marvelous!

WILLEM DE KOONING

You know what he can do? Blindfolded, he can throw two bowling balls at once down separate alleys and get two strikes. Now, that's what I call an artist!

TV

In late September 1958, I visited his South Truro studio and saw on the easel not an unfinished painting, nor even a stretched canvas, but a large empty stretcher. "He's been looking at that all summer." Jo Hopper said.

LLOYD GOODRICH OF EDWARD HOPPER

Once in a museum Bonnard persuaded his friend Vuillard to distract an attendant while he approached his own old painting, slipped from his pocket a tiny box of paints and a brush the size of a toothpick and added to one of his consecrated canvasses minute touches that set his mind at rest.

ANNETTE VAILLANT

When you get to the point where you cheat for the sake of beauty, you're an artist.

MAX JACOB

I unlearned to draw. The point was to forget with my hand.

MARCEL DUCHAMP

Our adventures tended toward the bizarre, like the day we met a blind man who took us to his home and introduced us to his family, all of whom were also blind. There was no light in the house, no lamps or candles, but on the walls hung a group of pictures of cemeteries. The pictures were made entirely of hair, right down to the tombs and the cypresses.

LUIS BUNUEL

The artist speaks to our capacity for delight and wonder; to the sense of mystery surrounding our lives; to our sense of pity, and beauty and pain; to the latent feeling of fellowship with creatures; to the subtle but invincible conviction of solidarity that knits together the loneliness of innumerable hearts; to the solidarity which binds together all humanity – the dead to the living and the living to the unborn.

JOSEPH CONRAD

Max Ernst said that collage is "the meeting of two distant realities on a plane foreign to them both."

The error begins the minute you take it into your head to buy a painting and a frame.

JOSEPH BUEYS

Artists don't talk about art. Artists talk about work. If I have any-thing to say to young writers, it's stop thinking of writing as art. Think of it as work. If you're an artist, whatever you do is going to be art. If you're not an artist, at least you can do a good days work. It's what you come in every morning to do. It's work. It's never art. Art is for academics. Art is for scholars. Art is for audiences. Art is not for artists.

PADDY CHAYEFSKY

Works of art can wait: indeed they do nothing but that and do it passionately.

RAINER MARIA RILKE

Does not all art come when a nature exhausts personal emotion in action or desire so completely that something impersonal, something that has nothing to do with action or desire, sudden-ly starts in its place, something which is as unforeseen, as com-pletely organized, even as unique, as the images that pass before the mind between sleeping and waking.

W.B. YEATS

Do not derive your art from art.

JEAN COCTEAU

Max Ernst used to describe how, as a child, he would watch his father painting in the back garden. One day Ernst Senior was stymied by a tree that he could not paint satisfactorily; so, to the outrage of his son the budding Surrealist, he fetched an axe and chopped it down, editing it from both life and art.

ROBERT HUGHES

The artist Leon Kroll was having trouble with a seascape. "My boy," said Winslow Homer, "if you want to make a great sea, use only two waves."

I can't think much of a people who drew cats the same for four thousand years.

LORD KITCHENER ON EGYPTIAN ART

Paul Valery said that modern artists want the grin without the cat.

Paul Cezanne averred he didn't need to take a vacation from painting his famous still lifes of fruit: he got all the excitement he could stand from the nuance of moving his easel a few inches.

Art is frozen Zen

R.H. BLYTH

No word meaning "art" occurs in Aivilik, nor does "artist;" there are only people. Nor is any distinction made between utilitarian and decorative objects. The Aivilik say simply, "A man should do all things properly." Art to the Aivilik is an act, not an object, a ritual, not a possession.

Technique is what is not learned.

PABLO PICASSO

A painter friend once praised a canvas he saw in Ryder's studio and was grateful to be offered it as a present. But after Ryder had washed the picture's face in a basin of very dirty water and dried it with a dirty towel, he stood gazing at it with a faraway look in his eyes, a look of fondest love. He had forgotten that I was there. When I gently recalled him to earth, he turned to me and with the simplicity of a child, said kindly and regretfully: "Come again next year and I think you can have it, if I find I can do what more it needs. I have only worked on it a little more than ten years."

ALEXANDER ELIOT

Works of art are of an infinite loneliness and with nothing so little to be reached as with criticism. Only love can grasp and hold and be just toward them.

RAINER MARIA RILKE

One always has to spoil a picture a little bit, in order to finish it.

EUGÈNE DELACROIX

When I have arranged a bouquet, in order to paint it I go around to the side that I have not looked at.

PIERRE AUGUSTE RENOIR

Once a friend found Rousseau painting with a wreath of leaves tied around the thumb that stuck through the palette; there were no leaves in the painting. The friend asked why he wore the bouquet. "One must study nature," said Rousseau.

ROGER SHATTUCK

I favor a picture which arrives at its destination without the evidence of a trying journey rather than the one which shows the marks of a battle.

CHARLES SHEELER

Hoyningen-Heune's close friends of the period are today universally known and respected: Gide, Jean Cocteau, Miro, Chanel, Poiret, Derain, Dali, Visconti and Berard. Of course none of them respected territorial rights in the arts. If an artist wasn't at his easel, he was busy writing films, or acting in them, or designing sets, curtains, fabrics, cars or new forms of typography.

WILLIAM EWING

You know, I have a theory about the decay of art in advanced civilizations. Perhaps it's a joke, but I believe it may be serious. It is that people want to make ugly things, but at the beginning their tools don't allow them to. When you find figures or vases in Mycenae or Guatemala or Peru, every one is a masterpiece. But when the perfection of technique allows men to do what they want, it is bad. Perfection of technique – sophistication – has nearly destroyed the movies.

JEAN RENOIR

It is impossible to make any distinction between a saw and the Parthenon. The Parthenon is as expendable as the saw is unique.

Walking one night along the boulevard Raspail with Gertrude Stein, Picasso saw a convoy of camouflaged artillery decked out in Cubist forms and color. "It is we that have created that," he told her proudly.

ARIANA HUFFINGTON

Alfred Barr challenged Duchamp's assertion that he had selected each readymade on the basis of visual indifference. "But, oh, Marcel," Barr said, "why do they look so beautiful today?" The reply was vintage Duchamp: "Nobody's perfect," he said.

In Paris, Rauschenberg met the American painter Sue Weil whom he later married. "We were scared of the concierge," Rauschenberg has recalled, "and whenever one of us spilled a drop of paint on the grimy old Oriental rug, we'd go around and carefully put a drop of the same color in several other places, to equalize it. After a while the room began to seem brighter and brighter."

CALVIN TOMKINS

Q. Do you believe that photography can be labeled art?
A. That is ridiculous and vain. Everything is art. A cook, a shoe-maker, a hairdresser are all artists according to how talented they are. This whole mess of labels and titles has nothing to do with me. I am absolutely indifferent to the noise and commotion. It isn't the medium that's important but the person that expresses himself through it. I just continue to look for those special moments, the way a fisherman does when he tells you, "They're biting today."

JACQUES HENRI LARTIGUE

I put the first brush stroke on the canvas. After that, it is up to the canvas to do at least half the work.

JAMES BROOKS

Aesthetics is for the artists like Ornithology is for the birds.

BARNETT NEWMAN

BREATHING ON YOUR OWN

There is no avant-garde. There are only people who are a little late.

EDGAR VARESE

I am for an art that is political-erotical-mystical, that does something other than sit on its ass in a museum.

CLAES OLDENBERG

The French painter Rousseau was once asked why he put a naked woman on a red sofa in the middle of one of his jungle pictures. He answered, "I needed a bit of red there."

What do they mean by religious art. It's an absurdity. How can you make religious art one day and another kind the next?

PABLO PICASSO

All day long I add up columns of figures and make everything balance. I come home. I sit down. I look at a Kandinsky and it's wonderful. It doesn't mean a damn thing!

SOLOMON GUGGENHEIM

Racing is strictly art for art's sake. There are few things more useless than a racecar.

SAM POSEY

The painter and the painter contemplating his painting are not the same man.

JOAN MIRO

Art does not come and lie in the beds we make for it. It slips away as soon as its name is uttered: it likes to preserve its incognito. Its best moments are when it forgets its very name.

JEAN DUBUFFET

His method is different; to live, speak, look at beautiful things together, to cultivate the soul without thinking of art – which in his eyes is no more than a margin of life.

JEAN MARAIS ABOUT JEAN COCTEAU

13

A man's work is nothing but this slow trek to rediscover, through the detours of art, those two or three great and simple images in whose presence his heart first opened.

ALBERT CAMUS

A portrait is a painting with something wrong with the mouth.

JOHN SINGER SARGENT

In art virtue is only a means placed at the service of risk.

ALBERT CAMUS

Art is a dialogue we have always carried out with the unknown.

ANDRE MALRAUX

All good art is an indiscretion.

TENNESSEE WILLIAMS

When I sit down to make a sketch from nature, the first thing I try to do is, to forget that I have ever seen a picture.

JOHN CONSTABLE

Do you still remember that time when painting was considered an end in itself? We have passed the period of individual exercises.

PAUL ELUARD

I perhaps owe having become a painter to flowers.

CLAUDE MONET

Picasso told me that he had seen in Avignon, on the square of the Chateau des Popes, an old painter, half-blind, who was painting the castle. His wife, standing beside him, looked at the castle through binoculars and described it to him. He was painting from his wife.

JEAN COCTEAU

An artist is a dreamer consenting to dream of the actual world.

GEORGE SANTAYANA

BREATHING ON YOUR OWN

How to paint the Landscape; First you make your bow to the Landscape. Then you wait and if and when the Landscape bows to you, then and not until then can you paint the Landscape.

JOHN MARIN

Delacroix said that one of the finest "paintings" he had ever seen was a particularly handsome Persian rug he once came across.

JOHN MARIN

We make things for somebody. This idea of art for art's sake is a hoax.

PABLO PICASSO

The artist is not a special kind of person; rather each person is a special kind of artist.

ANANDA COOMARASWAMY

You know, I like signing all those things. It devalues them.

MARCEL DUCHAMP

People are always talking about the Renaissance, but it's really pathetic. I've been seeing some Tintorettos recently. It's nothing but cinema, cheap cinema.

PABLO PICASSO

You must travel at random, like the first Mayans. You must risk getting lost in the thickets, but that is the only way to make art.

TEZCATILLIPOCA

For something to be a masterpiece you have to have enough time to talk when you have nothing to say.

JOHN CAGE

Among the languages of American Indians there is no word for "art". For Indians everything is art… therefore it needs no name.

JAMAKE HIGHWATER

At a performance of Pulcinello, Jean Hugo was sitting next to Picasso in Misia Sert's box. Suddenly, Picasso turned to him and asked: "So, are you still painting by hand?" Hugo would be puzzled by it for years.

It is more complete, looking out of windows in museums than looking out of windows anywhere else.

GERTRUDE STEIN

I don't want to be an artist strong in the picture. I wish I could obliterate the brushstrokes, the fact that it was done with human hands.

ANDREW WYETH

A mother and son visited the Seattle Art Museum. Several rooms were devoted to the work of Morris Graves. When they came to one in which all of the paintings were black, the mother, placing a hand across her son's eyes, said, "Come, dear, mother doesn't want you to see these things."

JOHN CAGE

When, for instance, you are painting a landscape, don't leave out the rain just because you've started with the sunshine.

HENRI MATISSE

Henri Matisse said that a drawing should have the decisiveness of a good sleep.

The brain must not interfere. You're painting so constantly that your brain disappears, and your subconscious goes into your fingers, and it just flows. If you think you're painting a good watercolor you can be sure it's lousy. It is important to forget what you are doing – then a work of art may happen.

ANDREW WYETH

BREATHING ON YOUR OWN

ATTENTION

Whatever the price, pay attention. Pay attention whatever price it asks. Otherwise you will pay through the nose for your non-attention.

JAMES BROUGHTON

I can never bring you to realize the importance of sleeves, the suggestiveness of thumb-nails, or the great issues that may hang from a bootlace.

SIR ARTHUR CONAN DOYLE

Look for a long time at what pleases you, and longer still at what pains you.

COLETTE

To perceive the truth, there must be a focusing of attention. This does not mean turning away from distraction. There is no such thing as distraction, because life is a movement and has to be understood as a total process.

KRISHNAMURTI

I promise to make you so alive that the fall of dust on furniture will deafen you.

NINA CASSIAN

So many things fail to interest us, simply because they don't find in us enough surfaces on which to live, and what we have to do then is to increase the number of planes in our mind, so that a much larger number of themes can find a place in it at the same time.

ORTEGA Y GASSET

My advice when watching movies is not to blink.

SISTER MARY CORITA.

Absolutely unmixed attention is prayer.

SIMONE WEIL

"You're not paying attention," said the Hatter. "If you don't pay him, you know, he won't perform."

LEWIS CARROLL

She is hard to tempt as everything seems to please her equally.

ANNE RAYMO

Be open, be available, be exposed, be skinless. Skinless? Dance around in your bones.

WALLACE STEGNER

Everything we come across is to the point.

JOHN CAGE

It is completely unimportant. That is why it is so interesting.

AGATHA CHRISTIE

No one can have an idea once he starts really listening.

JOHN CAGE

BEAUTIFUL/UGLY

Nobody ever discovered ugliness through photographs. Nobody exclaims, "Isn't that ugly! I must take a photograph of it." Even if someone did say that, all it would mean is: "I find that ugly thing beautiful!"

SUSAN SONTAG

In my best possible world, ugliness would be in museums, and everything out in the world, on the street, would be beautiful.

JOEL-PETER WITKIN

You have to run faster than beauty.

PABLO PICASSO

When beauty reaches great subtlety, the Japanese call the effect "Shibui" – restrained elegance.

When everyone recognizes beauty as beautiful, then there is ugliness. When everyone recognizes goodness as good, then there is evil.

ALAN WATTS

Suppose someone were to say "Imagine this butterfly exactly as it is but ugly instead of beautiful."

LUDWIG WITTGENSTEIN

Colette on her divan: "Oh! how I'd like to feel the cold belly of a little frog on each hand."

Beauty is about the improbable coming true suddenly.

CHARLES SIMIC

Without naivete, there is no beauty.

DIDEROT

BEGINNER

If the angel deigns to come, it will be because you have convinced him, not by tears, but by your humble resolve to be always beginning: to be a beginner.

RAINER MARIA RILKE

In the beginner's mind there is no thought, "I have attained something." All self-centered thoughts limit our vast mind. When we have no thought of achievement, no thought of self, we are true beginners. Then we can really learn something.

SHUNRYU SUZUKI

In Japan we have the phrase Shoshin, which means "beginner's mind." The goal of practice is always to keep our beginner's mind. Our "original mind" includes everything within itself. It is always rich and sufficient within itself. This does not mean a closed mind, but actually an empty mind and a ready mind. If your mind is empty, it is always ready for anything; it is open to everything. In the beginner's mind there are many possibilities; in the expert's mind there are few.

SHUNRYU SUZUKI

You have to wake up a virgin each morning.

JEAN-LOUIS BARRAULT

BELIEF

We believe as much as we can. We would believe everything if we could.

WILLIAM JAMES

The problem lies precisely in not accepting any explanation of the world either through chance or determinism. I am not responsible for my belief. It is not even I who decided that I am not responsible – and so on to infinity. I am not obliged to believe. There is no point of departure.

RENÉ MAGRITTE

And curious creatures that we are, in every sense of the word. Not only are we the sole animal in all of nature capable of believing in Santa Claus, we are also the only one that can come to grips with the unpleasant truth that he doesn't exist.

JON FRANKLIN

A visitor to Niels Bohr's country cottage, noticing a horseshoe hanging on the wall, teased the eminent scientist about this ancient superstition. "Can it be that you, of all people, believe it will bring you luck?" "Of course not," replied Bohr, "but I understand it brings you luck whether you believe or not."

I realized a long time ago that a belief which does not spring from a conviction in the emotions is no belief at all. When I am convinced of something, I an convinced with my whole self, as though my flesh had informed me. Knowledge is the condition of my being.

EVELYN SCOTT

"I don't believe," Duchamp said, "in the verb, to be. I do not believe that I am."

Suppose it were forbidden to say "I know" and only allowed to say "I believe I know"

LUDWIG WITTGENSTEIN

BIRDS

I am for the birds, not the cages that people put them in.

JOHN CAGE

Cuskoy, a town in eastern Turkey, is called the "bird village" with good reason. Its inhabitants have perfected a language system of chirps, tweets, and twitters almost indistinguishable from authentic bird sounds. The people of Cuskoy developed this unique system because of a ravine and a river which bisect their village and an almost daily fog that prevents the use of hand signals.

CHARLES BERLITZ

There's a strange frenzy in my head, of birds flying, each particle circulating on its own. Is the one I love everywhere?

RUMI

Only the birds are able to throw off their shadow. The shadow always stays behind on earth. Our imagination flies. We are its shadow on the earth.

VLADIMIR NABOKOV

Birds make great sky-circles of their freedom. How do they learn it? They fall, and falling, they're given wings.

RUMI

These birds do not learn to fly until they lose all their feathers.

RUMI

This is what the things can teach us: to fall, patiently to trust our heaviness. Even a bird has to do that before he can fly.

RAINER MARIA RILKE

Who knows? Perhaps the same bird echoed through both of us yesterday, separate, in the evening....

RAINER MARIA RILKE

CHANCE

Biologists have suggested that the universe, and the living forms it contains, are based on chance, but not on accident.

JEREMY CAMPBELL

Chance kills us all, eventually without choice.

There should be no promise of plot. Plot is extraordinary, while chance is ordinary.

JERZY KOSINSKI

When I was writing the Chorus in G Minor, I suddenly dipped my pen into the medicine bottle instead of the inkpot. I made a blot, and when I dried it with sand (blotting paper had not been invented then) it took the form of a natural, which instantly gave me the idea of the effect which the change from G Minor to G Major would make, and to this blot all the effect – if any – is due.

ROSSINI

There's less and less to do. Circumstances do it for us.

JOHN CAGE

Chance favors the prepared mind.

PASTEUR

We can't leave the haphazard to chance.

N. F. SIMPSON

My good friend Jacques Monod spoke often of the randomness of the cosmos. He believed everything in existence occurred by pure chance with the possible exception of his breakfast, which he felt certain was made by his housekeeper.

WOODY ALLEN

Coincidence, if traced far enough back, becomes inevitable.

HINEU

How to the invisible I hired myself to learn... that has as its last and seventh rule: the submission to chance.

CHARLES SIMIC

Beautiful, like the chance meeting of a sewing machine and an umbrella on a dissecting table.

COMTE DE LAUTREAMONT

A throw of the dice will never abolish chance.

MARCEL DUCHAMP

The immediate is chance. At the same time it is definitive. What I want is the definitive by chance.

JEAN-LUC GODARD

Your chance is not the same as mine, is it?

MARCEL DUCHAMP

Of the editing process Jean Cocteau said: "To reorganize chance."

CHANGE

Our only security is our ability to change.

YEHUDA AMICHAI

When a man changes he'll sign letters unread and let his photos develop forever, he'll order shoes and not take them, and he'll forget his coat in the wardrobe of strangers.

YEHUDA AMICHAI

It's time again. Tear up the violets and plant something more difficult to grow.

JAMES SCHUYLER

It was chilling to realize that the sentimental qualities most valued between people, like loyalty, constancy and affection, are the ones most likely to impede change.

TED SIMON

Everything in life that we really accept undergoes a change. So suffering must become love. That is the mystery.

KATHERINE MANSFIELD

Some people say about human beings, dust to dust, but can that be true of one who changes from road dust to doorway?

RUMI

The Duke of Cambridge protested that he wasn't against change. He favored it, he said, when there was no alternative.

This, then, is it: not the crude anguish of physical death, but the incomparable pangs of the mysterious mental maneuver needed to pass from one state of being to another. Easy, you know, does it, son.

VLADIMIR NABOKOV

The curious paradox is that when I accept myself just as I am, then I can change.

CARL ROGERS

Everything changes but the avant-garde.

PAUL VALERY

CHILD IN THE MAN

In my house I have put together a collection of small and large toys I can't live without. The child who doesn't play is not a child, but the man who doesn't play has lost forever the child who lived in him and he will certainly miss him. I have also built my house like a toyhouse and I play in it from morning till night.

PABLO NERUDA

It takes a very long time to become young.

PABLO PICASSO

(The complaints of the child in us) it will never cease lamenting until it is consoled, answered, understood. Only then will it lie still in us, like our fears. It will die in peace and leave us what the child leaves to the man – the sense of wonder.

ANAIS NIN

Self-actualizers are somehow both mature and childlike. They manifest "healthy childishness" and "a second naivete."

ABRAHAM MASLOW

All of us collect fortunes when we are children – a fortune of colors, of light and darkness, of movements, of tensions. Some of us have the fantastic chance to go back to their fortune when we grow up. Most of us don't have the chance - that is the tragedy.

INGMAR BERGMAN

Give me the madman's sudden insight and the child's spiritual dignity.

THEODORE ROETHKE

The poet is one who is able to keep the fresh vision of the child alive within the mature man.

ANAIS NIN

Matisse was accused of doing things any child could do, and he answered very cheerfully, "Yes, but not what you could do."

ALLAN KAPROW

The effort needed to see things without distortion takes something very like courage and this courage is essential to the artist, who has to look at everything as though he saw it for the first time: he has to look at life as he did when he was a child. If he loses that faculty, he cannot express himself in an original, that is, a personal way.

HENRI MATISSE

Well, I was out in L.A. recently on music business, and I was just sitting there in the office filling them in on some of my goals. And I said: "Listen, I've got a vision, I see myself as part of a long tradition of American humor. You know – Bugs Bunny, Daffy Duck, Porky Pig, Elmer Fudd, Roadrunner, Yosemite Sam." And they said: "Well actually we had something a little more adult in mind." And I said: "OK! OK! Listen, I can adapt!"

LAURIE ANDERSON

Kids: they dance before they learn there is anything that isn't music.

WILLIAM STAFFORD

There are children playing in the street who could solve some of my top problems in physics, because they have modes of sensory perception that I lost long ago.

J. ROBERT OPPENHEIMER

Grownups never understand anything by themselves, and it is tiresome for children to be always and forever explaining things to them.

ANTOINE DE SAINT-EXUPERY

No one shows a child the sky.

AFRICAN PROVERB

I can well understand why children love sand.

LUDWIG WITTGENSTEIN

When childhood dies its corpses are called adults.

BRIAN ALDIRA

A child has much to learn before it can pretend.

COMMUNICATION

Any means of communication which can be unplugged cannot be independent.

JOHN RALSTON SAUL

And Satie... I can tell you something about him that will perhaps seem only amusing. But it is very significant. He had died, and we all went to his apartment, and under his blotter on his desk we all found our letters to him – unopened.

JEAN COCTEAU

This has been a most wonderful evening. Gertrude has said things tonight it'll take her ten years to understand.

ALICE B. TOKLAS

Researchers at Bell Laboratories estimate that there is more information in a weekly edition of The New York Times than a person in the sixteenth century processed in a lifetime.

LAWRENCE SHAINBERG

Ignore previous cookie.

(MESSAGE IN FORTUNE COOKIE)

Nothing would astonish me, after all these years, except to be understood.

ELLEN GLASGOW

When I was born I was so surprised I didn't talk for a year and a half.

GRACIE ALLEN

The rules are simple – start on dry land, finish on dry land.

MIKE READ, KING OF THE ENGLISH CHANNEL

Q. Thomas Edison lost much of his hearing at an early age. But I just read he and his wife attended stage plays. How did he hear the actors? A. His wife fingertipped key lines of dialogue in Morse Code on his knee. Didn't I tell you he taught her Morse code? Then tapped out his marriage proposal in her hand? She tapped back her acceptance.

NEWSPAPER

So my voice becomes both a breath and a shout. One prepares the way, the other surrounds my loneliness with angels.

RAINER MARIA RILKE

No one would think of keeping a (musical) chord to himself. You'd give it to anyone who wanted it.

JOHN CAGE

CONCENTRATION

One must bear in mind one thing. It isn't necessary to know what that thing is.

JOHN ASHBERY

I was once given advice by an Indian who was very much worried about my preoccupation with words. "You must learn to look at the world twice," he told me as I sat on the floor of his immaculately swept adobe room. "First you must bring your eyes together in front so you can see each droplet of rain on the grass, so you can see the smoke rising from an anthill in the sunshine. Nothing should escape your notice. But you must learn to look again, with your eyes at the very edge of what is visible. Now you must see dimly if you wish to see things that are dim-visions, mist, and cloud-people... animals which hurry past you in the dark. You must learn to look at the world twice if you wish to see all that there is to see."

JAMAKE HIGHWATER

Concentrate, don't embroider.

SPENCER TRACY

...only that our eye would have to be a trace more seeing, our ear more receptive, the taste of a fruit would have to penetrate us more completely, we would have to endure more odor, and in touching and being touched be more aware and less forgetful.

RAINER MARIA RILKE

When we came in she had her chair sideways by the window looking out at the snow, and she said, without even looking up to know that it was us, that the doctor had said that sitting and staring at the snow was a waste of time. She should get involved in something. She laughed and told us it wasn't a waste of time. It would be a waste of time just to stare at snowflakes but she was counting, and even that might be a waste of time, but she was only counting the ones that were just alike.

ANN BEATTIE

Concentration is not to try hard to watch something. In zazen if you try to look at one spot you will be tired in about five minutes. This is not concentration. Concentration means freedom. So your effort should be directed at nothing. You should be concentrated on nothing.

SUZUKI

BREATHING ON YOUR OWN

It involves looking at everything one wants to describe long enough, and attentively enough, to find in it some aspect that no one has yet seen or expressed. Everything contains some element of the unexplored because we are accustomed to use our eyes only with the memory of what other people before us have thought about the object we are looking at. In order to describe a fire burning or a tree in the field, let us stand in front of that fire and that tree until they no longer look to us like any other fire or any other tree.

GUY DE MAUPASSANT

During the siege of silence, Marlon Brando located a letter buried among the dinner plates, and read it while he ate, like a gentlemen perusing his breakfast newspaper. Presently, remembering me, he remarked "From a friend of mine. He's making a documentary, the life of James Dean. He wants me to do the narration. I think I might." He tossed the letter aside and pulled his apple pie, topped with a melting scoop of vanilla ice cream, toward him. "Maybe not though. I get excited about something but it never lasts more than seven minutes. Seven minutes exactly. That's my limit. I never know why I get up in the morning."

TRUMAN CAPOTE

For the things whose essential life you want to express, begin by asking "Are you free? Are you prepared to devote all your love to me?" And if the thing sees that you are preoccupied, with even a mere particle of your interest, it shuts itself up again; it may perhaps give you a counter-sign, it may make a little, faintly friendly sign but it refuses to give you its heart, to disclose to you its patient being, its sweet sidereal constancy that makes it so like the constellations. If a thing is to speak to you, you must regard it for a certain time as the only one that exists, as the one and only phenomenon, which, thanks to your laborious and exclusive love, is now placed at the center of the Universe, and there, in that incomparable place, is this day attended by the Angels.

RAINER MARIA RILKE

30

CONFUSION

"Nothing," said Moon. "I was trying to face one way or the other and I got confused and fell over. Let that be my epitaph."

TOM STOPPARD

Feeling that he must run and that he will take root forever and stand, does both at once and neither, grows blind, and then sees everything, steps and becomes a man of stars instead.

JAMES DICKEY

The best things can't be said. The second best are misunderstood.

HEINRICH ZIMMER

I have a feeling that my boat has struck, down there in the depths, against a great thing. And nothing happens! Nothing... Silence... Waves... Nothing happens! Or has everything happened, and are we standing now, quietly, in the new life?

JUAN RAMON JIMENEZ

Now I don't know which way to be. Absent-minded or respectful.

PABLO NERUDA

It is as if these colors took away all your indecisions forever and ever.

RAINER MARIA RILKE

This ghost-ridden, tacitly comic man, dedicated to the noble structure of accuracy, responded at once to a mention of Brecht's poems. He answered, "They are optimistic when I am sad. They are written from a standpoint of not being certain, and it's a very good way to convince. They say that the world is not sad, it is big."

PENELOPE GILLIATT ON JEAN-LUC GODARD

Basic research is what I am doing when I don't know what I am doing.

WERNER VON BRAUN

CONSCIOUS/UNCONSCIOUS

Neurophysiologists will not likely find what they are looking for outside their own consciousness, for that which they are looking for is that which is looking.

KEITH FLOYD

The conscious mind is the editor, and the unconscious mind is the writer.

DAVID MAMET

Giulietta, my wife, has the gift for evoking a kind of waking dream quite spontaneously, as if it were taking place quite outside her own consciousness. She embodies in our relationship my nostalgia for innocence.

FEDERICO FELLINI

Toward the end of his life, Rainer Maria Rilke began to describe the new powers - moving from one part of the brain to another, leaping quickly from conscious to unconscious – as if they were a new power in listening. it's an amazing idea. He imagines the road not as if it's a road over the sea but as if it were a thread of sound.

From Anton Webern's Cantata No. 2 – listen to the opening words of the second section, and remember Webern was writing in one of the worst periods (1941-43) in human history: "Keep deep down," the poem says, "for the innermost life sings in the hive." And it's not the name on the hive that matters either. It's the keeping deep down, and the way the honey tastes.

JOHN RUSSELL

How it is that anything so remarkable as a state of consciousness comes about as a result of irritating nervous tissue, is just as unaccountable as the appearance of the Djin, when Aladdin rubbed his lamp.

THOMAS HUXLEY

COURAGE

We all need a little more courage now and then. That's what I
need. If you have some to share, I want to know you. Your criti-
cisms you can keep to yourselves.

MARVIN BELL

Perhaps all the dragons of our lives are princesses who are only
waiting to see us once beautiful and brave.

RAINER MARIA RILKE

Among the many legends that surround the Nepalese Gurkhas
of the British Army is the story of a paratroop regiment in the
Second World War. The leader of the regiment asked for volunteers for a particularly dangerous drop behind enemy lines.
About half the Gurkhas promptly stepped forward. The leader
then went through what the volunteers would be asked to do.
Halfway into his explanation, a surprised voice piped up from
the back: "Oh, you mean we can use parachutes?" Every
remaining Gurkha joined the volunteers.

RADIO TIMES, LONDON

If there is one door in the castle you have been told not to go
through, you must. Otherwise you'll just be rearranging furniture
in rooms you've already been in.

ANNE LAMOTT

The essence of spirit, he thought to himself, was to choose the
thing which did not better one's position, but made it more per-
ilous. That was why the world he knew was poor, for it insisted
morality and caution were identical.

D.H. LAWRENCE

We must assume our existence as broadly as we in any way
can; everything, even the unheard-of, must be possible in it. That
is, at bottom, the only courage that is demanded of us.

RAINER MARIA RILKE

She dreamed that she was commanded to descend into "A pit filled with hot stuff" and immerse herself in it. This she did, till only one shoulder was sticking out of the pit. Then Jung came along, pushed her right down into the hot stuff, exclaiming "Not out but through."

ANIELA JAFFE

Beyond a certain point there is no return. This point has to be reached.

FRANZ KAFKA

He opens himself to all influences – everything nourishes him. Everything is gravy to him, including what he does not understand – particularly what he does not understand.

HENRY MILLER

If I can't take what happens, I'm not ready for anything.

JOHN CAGE

CREATIVITY

In some basic way, I have always really felt in my more rational and intelligent moments that there is something tremendously creative about truancy.

JONATHAN MILLER

Man consumes himself by his creation. There was a famous episode in a Marx Brothers film in which the brothers steal a train, the train runs out of coal and they begin breaking up the carriages and piling them into the fire; finally they break up the engine itself and push it into the furnace, until the train is only a furnace on wheels. This describes Yeats' conception of the working of the creative faculty.

COLIN WILSON

BREATHING ON YOUR OWN

In an ingenious set of experiments, Brandeis University Professor Teresa Amabile has shown that creativity itself may depend on the intrinsic nature of absorption, that is, it depends on being its own reward. Amabile tested subjects ranging from children to undergraduate women, rewarding some of them for creative tasks. Their creative productions were then rated by a panel of judges composed of professional creators. Amabile and the colleagues report that no matter what the reward was or when it was given, if the subjects thought they were working for an external remuneration, they became less creative.

Anyone can look for fashion in a boutique or history in a museum. The creative person looks for history in a hardware store and fashion in an airport.

ROBERT WIEDER

Creativity "is the retention throughout life of something that belongs properly to infant experience. I mean seeing everything afresh all the time... When we are surprised at ourselves, we are being creative, and we find we can trust our own unexpected originality." (he is talking of cooking sausages)

D.W. WINNICOTT

All great work is preparing yourself for the accident to happen.

SYDNEY LUMET

According to The Oxford English Dictionary, the word "creativity" didn't appear in print until 1875.

DENISE SHEKERJIAN

In order to be created, a work of art must first of all make use of the dark forces of the soul. But not without channeling them, surrounding them with dikes, so that the water in them rises. (a great garden of silence).

ALBERT CAMUS

John Keats pointed out a basic requirement for creativity: empathy, openness, the ability to take in or become the whole world.

The best part of one's life is the working part, the creative part. Believe me, I love to succeed. However the real spiritual and emotional excitement is in the doing.

GARSON KANIN

This afternoon I did not want to see an unknown gentleman, but coming out of the house, I find the gentleman still waiting, hoping to see me all the same. I talk to him and learn that he is by profession a whalesman. Immediately, the same instant, I request him to send me several vertebrae of this mammal. He has promised to do so with the utmost diligence. My capacity to profit from everything is unlimited. In less than an hour I have listed sixty-two different applications for these whale vertebrae – a ballet, a film, a painting, a philosophy, a therapeutic decoration, a magical effect, a hallucinatory method both Lilliputian and psychological because of its so-called phantasies of grandeur, a morphological law, proportions exceeding human measurement, a new way to pee, a brush. All this in the shape of a whale's vertebrae.

SALVADOR DALI

If you take any activity, any art, any discipline, any skill, take it and push it as far as it will go, push it beyond where it has ever been before, push it to the wildest edge of edges, then you force it into the realm of magic.

TOM ROBBINS

After dinner, blew soap-bubbles with much success. From one bubble, I formed as many as forty or fifty little bubbles. This game is truly poetic. It demands much sleight-of-hand. Sept. 24, 1679 (3 p.m.)

AMIEL'S JOURNAL.

When creators conceive of simultaneous opposites, they're not flipping from one opposition to another or even resolving the opposites into a synthesis or reconciliation of opposites. The thinking is quite different because it may consist of a paradox which is intrinsically unresolvable, unreconcilable, and unsusceptible to synthesis.

JOHN BRIGGS

It all began with my "eye-trapper" when I was a little boy. I used to close my eyes and turn around three times. I believed that way I could trap the air, the scents, the life that surrounded me. The trap didn't work very well, but I never got over the idea of it.

JACQUES HENRI LARTIGUE

To discard the unnecessary requires courage and also extra hard work, as exemplified by Pascal's effort to explain an idea to a friend in a letter which rambled on for pages and ended, "I am sorry to have wearied you with so long a letter but I did not have time to write you a short one."

BARBARA TUCHMAN

Not any self-control or self-limitation for the sake of specific ends, but rather a carefree letting go of oneself; not caution, but rather a wise blindness; not working to acquire silent, slowly increasing possessions, but rather a continuous squandering of all perishable values.

RAINER MARIA RILKE

To make creative breakthroughs, or, as Buckminster Fuller called them, intuitively inadvertent cul-de-sacs.

Everybody has a given amount of calories to burn up - you either burn them up by living or by creating. You can't burn the same calories both ways. You make poetry out of your unhappiness, and you might argue that you can also make poetry out of your happiness. But why should you make poetry when you are happy instead of living it out? Creativity is a secondary expression. The primary expression is living.

ARTHUR KOESTLER

Perhaps I know to what extent I can go too far.

JEAN COCTEAU

One must stop before one has finished.

BARBARA TUCHMAN

If the butterflies in your stomach die, send yellow death announcements.

YOKO ONO

I make all my decisions on intuition. But then, I must know why I made that decision. I throw a spear into the darkness. That is intuition. Then I must send an army into the darkness to find the spear. That is intellect.

INGMAR BERGMAN

In order to compose, all you need do is remember a tune that no one else has thought of.

ROBERT SCHUMANN

It is a tremendous act of violence to begin anything. I am not able to begin. I simply skip what should be the beginning.

RAINER MARIA RILKE

Genius is not having enough talent to do it the way it has been done before.

JAMES BROUGHTON

But I? Do I not depend on making angels, things, animals, even monsters when necessary, precisely out of that which could not be lived because it was too huge, too premature, too horrible?

RAINER MARIA RILKE

First, I write down all I know about the story, at length and in detail. Then I sink the iceberg and let some of it float up just a little.

INGMAR BERGMAN

If I find a film dull, I find it infinitely more entertaining to watch the scratches.

NORMAN MCLAREN

CULTURE

When the Nandi men are away on a foray, nobody at home may pronounce the names of the absent warriors; they must be referred to as birds.

SIR JAMES FRAZER

Father Michaellod was horrified to find his New Guinea native parishioners all preferred hell to heaven. It took him some time to find out why. On the mission picture, hell was depicted as a place of eternal fire, peopled by dark-skinned beings with spear-like pitchforks. Heaven, on the other hand, was depicted as a place of cloud and mist, among which many white people stood, pale and menacing.

TIM FLANNERY

You see, when weaving a blanket, an Indian woman leaves a flaw in the weaving of that blanket to let the soul out.

MARTHA GRAHAM

In a paper presented by John Wilson of the African Institute of London University, Wilson describes how the members of a primitive African village were shown a film intended to teach them methods of sanitation. To Wilson's surprise, not one of the thirty odd villagers watching the film were able to see it. When questioned about what they had seen the villagers were unable to answer except for the curious fact that they had all seen a chicken that had made a momentary appearance in the film.

In the Highlands of New Guinea I saw men with photographs of themselves mounted on their heads.

TED CARPENTER

Some modern hunter-gatherers, such as the San of Namibia, and Australian aborigines, draw certain animals that are "good to think" rather than good to eat.

LEONARD KRISHTALKA

There was a song for goin' to China and a song for goin' to Japan, a song for the big island and a song for the smaller one. All she had to know was the song and she knew where she was. To get back, she just sang the song in reverse. (an old Naotka woman describes how her forebears would navigate their ocean going canals.)

BRUCE CHATWIN

In Tanna Tuva, I show a movie of Pudovkin. The peasants got very upset and agitated at one point in the film. Finally, I realized it was because of the close-ups. "We paid full price and we expect to see full people. Why are we being shown only a part of a person."

RICHARD FEYNMAN

On a hot day in the southern desert of Africa I had wanted to go and speak to one of my favorite Stone Age hunters. He was sitting in the middle of a thorn bush. He was huddled in an attitude of the most intense concentration... but his friends would not let me get near him, saying, "But don't you know, he is doing work of the utmost importance. He is making clouds."

LAURENS VAN DER POST

About the Tarahumara Indians of the Southwest Sierra Madre: After he dies, every Tarahumara must make a journey to every place he ever lived and gather his footprints so that he can present them, along with his hair, to God.

ALEX SHOUNATOFF

While superintending Pueblo pottery revivals, Kenneth Chapman of the museum of New Mexico insisted that Maria Martinez authenticate and increase the value of her pottery by signing it – something that Pueblo potters had never done. When the other potters in the village realized that pots with Maria's signature commanded higher prices, they asked her to sign their pots as well and she freely did so until the Santa Fe authorities realized what was happening and put an end to it.

BREATHING ON YOUR OWN

As one scholar aptly put it, in many non-Western cultures they "don't tell you what time it is; they tell you what kind of time it is."

BROD TECHNOSTRUS

DAY/NIGHT

The afternoon knows what the morning never suspected.

SWEDISH PROVERB

We burn daylight.

WILLIAM SHAKESPEARE

For one moment, sleep the human night. Light your four-sided constellation in me.

PABLO NERUDA

Come even so. We will start. Bring your nights with you.

W. S. MERWIN

Yet I think I know your turning sigh and your trusting arm's abandonment, for they are the picture of my night.

FROM THE ARABIC OF JOHN DUNCAN

How long the sun and moon have been turning day and night, just to spend one night with You!

RUMI

We have our hands to entwine. Nothing can ever seduce better than our attachment one to the other forest giving earth back to sky and sky to night. To night which prepares an endless day.

PAUL ELUARD

Night and morning are making promises to each other which neither will be able to keep.

RICHARD SHELTON

41

At the hour when neither day or night knows more than the other. At the hour when day and night do not know that there is a sharing.

LOUIS EMIE

The night is trying to teach the day how to pretend.

Actually, light dazzles me. I keep only enough of it in me to look at night, the whole night, all nights.

PAUL ELUARD

I got lost in the night, without the light of your eyelids, and when the night surrounded me I was born again. I was the owner of my own darkness.

PABLO NERUDA

The day is emptying its pockets, laying out, one by one, all its possessions.

JANOS PILINSZKY

If I had planned it, I should never have made the sun at all. See! How beautiful! The sun is too bright and too hot. And if there were only the moon there would be no reading and writing.

LUDWIG WITTGENSTEIN

To me that means unraveling a day thread by thread, seam by seam; the whole pattern dissolves into long threads, all the work pours back into my hands, and I begin a difficult, a reproachful night.

RAINER MARIA RILKE

DEATH

When I die, I will not see myself die, for the first time.

ANTONIO PORCHIA

Death, fumbling to uncover my body in his bed, shall know there has been one before him.

Elegy: who would I show it to?

W.S. MERWIN

Death is not in the nature of things: it is the nature of things.

We are attempting to communicate, but no communication between us can abolish our fundamental difference. If you die, it is not my death.

GEORGES BATAILLE

We watch things pass by in order to forget that they are watching us die.

ROBBE-GRILLET

Dying of not dying....

PAUL ELUARD

By daily dying I have come to be.

THEODORE ROETHKE

I am a teacher of life and a vague student of death.

PABLO NERUDA

Death is patiently making my mask as I sleep. Each morning I awake to discover in the corners of my eyes the small tears of his wax.

PHILIP DOW

We do survive every moment, after all, except the last one.

JOHN UPDIKE

Poetry will rob me of my death.

RENÉ CHAR

It is impossible to experience one's own death objectively and still carry a tune.

WOODY ALLEN

For a long time I have been preparing myself for the exercise which consists, for the poet, in simulating death.

JEAN COCTEAU

If death can fly, just for the love of flying, what might not life do, for the love of dying?

MALCOLM LOWRY

I don't want to die, I want to watch cartoons.

STEPHEN BERG'S DAUGHTER

It is not the failed relationships which influence our life – they influence our death.

ANAIS NIN

Here I am trying to live, or rather, I am trying to teach the death within me how to live.

JEAN COCTEAU

I wonder if, before we were born, we were as afraid of life as we are now of death.

JAY WILLIAMS

The great courage is still to gaze as squarely at the light as at death.

ALBERT CAMUS

We will gather images and images of images up till the last, which is blank. This one we will agree on.

EDMOND JABES

BREATHING ON YOUR OWN

The thing to remember is that each time of life has its appropriate rewards, whereas when you're dead it's hard to find the light switch.

WOODY ALLEN

That which we die for lives as wholly as that which we live for dies.

E.E.CUMMINGS

You are not afraid to die. Why are you afraid to live?

JOANNA SPARKS

I have died so little today, friend, forgive me.

THOMAS LUX

Between lips and voice, something went off to die; something with bird's wings, something of anguish and forgetting. Like nets which can't hold water.

PABLO NERUDA

I wish I could have known earlier that you have all the time you'll need right up to the day you die.

WILLIAM WILEY

There's an excellent profile in Interview magazine in which Jeanne Moreau says: "I shall die very young." "How young?" they ask her? "I don't know... maybe seventy, maybe eighty, maybe ninety. But I shall be very young."

BY WAY OF DIANA VREELAND

Die in your thoughts every morning and you will no longer fear death.

HAGAKURE

Until death, it is all life.

CERVANTES

While I thought I was learning how to live, I have been learning how to die.

LEONARDO DA VINCI

So much of adolescence is an ill-defined dying.

THEODORE ROETHKE

"If you love something well enough," grandmother Archa told Helen when the weakness was upon her, "you will die for it. For when we love with all our might, our silly little selves are already dead and we have no more fear of dying." "Would you die for your music?" Helen asked. And her grandmother said: "I believe I already have."

WILLIAM KENNEDY

If my doctor told me I only had six months to live, I wouldn't brood. I'd type a little faster.

ISAAC ASIMOV

To be blessed in death, one must learn to live. To be blessed in life, one must learn to die.

JESUIT VERSE

To live several lives, you have to die several deaths.

FRANÇOISE GIROUD

Death is just infinity closing in.

JORGE LUIS BORGES

While living, be a dead man, be thoroughly dead – and behave as you like, and all's well.

ZEN MASTER BUNAN

Give me your mouth so I can die on your lips.

RUMI

Why are you afraid of death? Where you are, death is not. Where death is, you are not. What is it that you fear.

EPICURIUS

"When I told him that he had only eight months to live," the doctor repeated to his colleagues with a sense of wonder, "he gave a great sigh of relief. 'This was' he said, 'the first time he had such solid assurance.'"

BEREL LANG

"Tell them that death is absolutely safe." And then he added, "It's like taking off a tight shoe."

PAT RODEGAST, IN CONTACT WITH A DISEMBODIED BEING NAMED EMMANUEL

You think you are killing me. I think you are committing suicide.

ANTONIO PORCHIA

If every death (like every life) has been allotted a certain portion of time, then days like the last ones will have to be counted up and deducted from its sum.

RAINER MARIA RILKE

Be absolute for death; either death or life shall thereby be the sweeter.

SHAKESPEARE

How fascinating the idea of death can be. Too bad, though because it just isn't true.

HAFIZ

If I had my life over again I should form the habit of nightly composing myself to thoughts of death. I would practice, as it were, the remembrance of death. There is no other practice which so intensifies life. Without an ever-present sense of death life is insipid. You might as well live on the whites of eggs.

MURIEL SPARK

You could see him walking alone with Her, unafraid of her scythe.

ANTONIO MACHADO

We will never have any memory of dying.

PABLO NERUDA

To die more fully, if dying is what must be done.

GUILLEVIC

The Friend, who knows a lot more than you do, will bring difficulties, and grief, and sickness, as medicine, as happiness, as the essence of the moment when you're beaten when you hear Checkmate, and can finally say, I trust you to kill me.

RUMI

This is the way to die: beauty keeps laying its sharp knife against me.

HAFIZ

Death is not an event in life.   .

LUDWIG WITTGENSTEIN

There are so many little dyings that it doesn't matter which of them is death.

KENNETH PATCHEN

DESIRE/LONGING

Sharp nostalgia, infinite and terrible, for what I already possess.

JUAN RAMON JIMENEZ

I do not know how to leap from the shore of today to the shore of tomorrow. The river carries, meanwhile, the reality of this evening to forlorn and hopeless seas.

BREATHING ON YOUR OWN

And it is always the same confession, the same youth, the same pure eyes, the same ingenuous gesture of her arms about my neck, the same caress, the same revelation. But it is never the same woman. The cards have said that I would meet her in life, but without recognizing her.

PAUL ELUARD

I am homesick for a country. I have never been there. I shall never go there. But where the clouds remember me distinctly.

HILDE DOMIN

To the sea? To the sky? To the world? Who knows? The stars descend, as usual to the river, carried by the breezes... the nightingale meditates... sorrow grows more lovely. And high above sadness a smile bursts into bloom.

JUAN RAMON JIMENEZ

Yet some things you miss and some things you lose by keeping your arm outstretched.

Long only for what you have.

ANDRE GIDE

And I say to reassure myself: desires are the memories from our future.

RAINER MARIA RILKE

Even things divulge the form of their desires if we could read their lips. Everything that is reflected in a window or a polished surface is being judged for its likeness to a glacier, which may never have existed.

W. S. MERWIN

When you read these lines, think of me and of what I have not written here.

ADRIENNE RICH

You, my own deep soul, trust me. I will not betray you. My blood is alive with many voices telling me I am made of longing.

RAINER MARIA RILKE

DESPAIR

If you are depressed, you are too high up in your mind.

CARL JUNG

We laughed at the hollyhocks together and then I sprayed them with lye. Forgive me. I simply do not know what I am doing.

KENNETH KOCH

I have a sailboat of sinking water.

ANONYMOUS CHILD

If you are still alive when you read this, close your eyes. I am under their lids, growing black.

SAINT GERAUD

It seems unlikely that the possibilities of continually undermining one's assumptions can go on unfolding indefinitely... without being eventually checked by despair or by a laugh that leaves one without any breath at all.

SUSAN SONTAG

Crops like mine are not so much planted as buried.

PETER DAVISON

A perfect, paralyzing bliss contented as despair.

EMILY DICKINSON

He who has seen everything empty itself is close to knowing what everything is filled with.

ANTONIO PORCHIA

Never mind. The self is the least of it. Let our scars fall in love.

GALWAY KINNELL

DETACHMENT

What I most want is to spring out of this personality, then to sit apart from that leaping. I've lived too long where I can be reached.

RUMI

At last I have become detached from every single natural thing.

GUILLAUME APOLLINAIRE

And all never-belonging be yours!

RAINER MARIA RILKE

I used to want buyers for my work. Now I wish someone would buy me away from words. I'm so tired of what I've been doing. Then one image without form came, and I quit. Look for someone else to mend the shop. I'm out of the image-making business. Only love. Only the holder the flag fits into, and wind. No flag.

RUMI

Clarity. I think I am coming toward you, I bear myself with such indifference.

JON ANDERSON

All I know is that he kept what he had by leaving it.

DREAMS

I have spread my dreams under your feet: tread softly because you tread on my dreams.

W.B. YEATS

Deserve your dream.

OCTAVIO PAZ

Imagine that you're dreaming.

ROBERT GRAVES

While we are asleep in this world, we are awake in another one.

JORGE LUIS BORGES

I will dive quietly into your sleeping and kiss your eyelids from within.

RAINER MARIA RILKE

You are always telling a dream. When do you dream it?

ANTONIO PORCHIA

Call it a dream. It does not change anything.

LUDWIG WITTGENSTEIN

The last Japanese character written in this life by Soen Roshi's venerable teacher, and the last word spoken, was the word for "dream."

In dreams begin responsibilities.

W.B. YEATS

The atoms and molecules within you dream they are people. How real their dream is to you! How deep a trance is your life!

FROM THE SETH TAPES

Sipping the cold soup made from the chrysanthemums of dreams.

PAUL CARROLL

When I am asleep I dream what I dream when I am awake. It is a continuous dream.

ANTONIO PORCHIA

Now, in the exacting twilight, to choose, not what we shall do or how we shall live but to choose the life whose dreams will hurt least in the nights to come.

YEHUDA AMICHAI

Sleep faster. We need the pillows.

YIDDISH PROVERB

When we dream that we dream, we are beginning to wake up.

NOVALIS

We don't learn the word "dream" by being shown a dream, the way we learn the word "apple" by being shown an apple.

In my dream, I am your customer, and the customer is always right.

LAURIE ANDERSON

Dreams are not made to put us to sleep, but to awaken us.

GOEMANS

Reality can destroy the dream, why shouldn't the dream destroy reality?

GEORGE MOORE

I cannot say I was hostile to him, nor friendly either: I have never dreamed of him.

GEORG CHRISTOPH LICHTENBERG

The key to success is simple. Make people dream.

GÉRARD DE NERVAL

I am the dream you are dreaming. When you want to awaken, I am that wanting.

RAINER MARIA RILKE

We dream in order to forget.

FRANCIS CRICK

I do not ask of God that he should change anything in events themselves, but that he should change me in regard to things, so that I might have the power to create my own universe, to govern my dreams, instead of enduring them.

GÉRARD DE NERVAL

I was not looking for my dreams to interpret my life, but rather for my life to interpret my dreams.

SUSAN SONTAG

It's useless to play lullabies for those who cannot go to sleep.

JOHN CAGE

All the things one has forgotten scream for help in dreams.

ELIAS CANETTI

Man sees and moves in what he sees, but he sees only what he dreams.

PAUL VALERY

Those who have likened our life to a dream were more right, by chance, than they realized. We are awake sleeping, and sleep awake.

MONTAIGNE

And he (Yeats) tells us that Shaw appeared to him in a dream in the form of a sewing machine, "that clicked and shone, but the incredible thing was that the machine smiled, smiled perpetually."

EDMUND WILSON

One does not dream; one is dreamed. We undergo the dream, we are the objects.

CARL JUNG

BREATHING ON YOUR OWN

I remember a medicine man in Africa who said to me almost with tears in his eyes: "We have no dreams anymore since the British are in the country." When I asked him why, he answered: "The District Commissioner knows everything."

CARL JUNG

Only the dreamer can change the dream.

JOHN LOGAN

The "rebound" effect usually shows very clearly when dream-deprived people have the chance to sleep normally but Vincent Zancone and his colleagues at Stanford University found that it did not occur in schizophrenic patients. It was as if they had enough dreaming while awake.

NIGEL CALDER

Ah in that minute, my dear, a dream with its terrible wings was covering you.

PABLO NERUDA

In relief, in humiliation, in terror, he understood that he, too, was an appearance, that someone else was dreaming him.

JORGE LUIS BORGES

Dreams are real while they last, can we say more of life?

HAVELOCK ELLIS

Not to dream boldly may turn out to be simply irresponsible.

GEORGE LEONARD

For the womb has dreams. It is not as simple as the good earth.

ANAIS NIN

We have to sleep with open eyes, we must dream with our hands.

OCTAVIO PAZ

...a good billiard table, a rowing boat, a wife, or some other dream of bliss.

GUSTAVE FLAUBERT

EGO

I very much doubt if anyone of us has the faintest idea of what is meant by the reality of existence of anything but our own egos.

A. EDDINGTON

There's nothing to believe. Only when I quit believing in myself did I come into This Beauty.

RUMI

The ingenuities we practice in order to appear admirable to ourselves would suffice to invent the telephone twice over on a rainy summer morning.

BRENDAN GILL

Every time you are near Him you have to leave pieces of your ego with the hatcheck girl who won't give them back.

HAFIZ

I have on my wall a great quote from Sir Laurence Olivier. He and Charlton Heston had done a play somewhere about 25 years ago, and they'd gotten slaughtered. Heston said, "Well, I guess you've just got to forget the bad reviews." And Olivier said, "No, you've got to forget the good ones."

WILLIAM GOLDMAN

ENLIGHTENMENT

"Enlightenment," a Zen Master has said, "is simply this: when I walk, I walk. When I eat, I eat. When I sleep, I sleep."

In the poetry contest in China by which the Sixth Patriarch of Zen Buddhism was chosen, there were two poems. One said: "The mind is like a mirror. It collects dust. The problem is to remove the dust." The other and winning poem was actually a reply to the first. It said, "Where is the mirror and where is the dust?" Some centuries later in a Japanese monastery there was a monk who was always taking baths. A younger monk came up to him and said, "Why, if there is no dust, are you always taking baths?" The older monk replied, "Just a dip. No why."

JOHN CAGE

If the place I want to arrive at could only be reached by a ladder, I would give up trying to arrive at it. For the place I really have to reach is where I must already be.

LUDWIG WITTGENSTEIN

But what is letting go? I think we don't understand it at all. We've got this idea of something trapped that we've got to set free. Like there's a bird in your hand, and what Zen is about is spreading your fingers and letting it fly away. Whoosh, I'm enlightened! But you and the bird are the same! You and your hand are the same! Nothing needs to be opened! Nothing needs to fly away! Realize this and you've automatically let go.

LAWRENCE SHAINBERG

Existence is no more than a flaw in the perfection of non-existence.

PAUL VALERY

The Zen monk Bassui wrote a letter to one of his disciples who was about to die, and in it he said: "Your end which is endless is as a snowflake dissolving in the pure air." The snowflake, which was once very much a discernible subsystem of the universe, now dissolves into the larger system which once held it. Though it is no longer present as a distinct subsystem, its essence is somehow present, and will remain so. It floats in Tumbolia, along with hiccups that are not being hiccuped and characters in stories that are not being read.

DOUGLAS HOFSTADER

To understand is almost the opposite of existing.

GEORGES POULET

As for myself, ever since I was born on November 5th, 1926, I have struggled with my puzzling conviction that everything is simultaneous.

JOHN BERGER

FAILURE/SUCCESS

It goes without saying that as soon as one cherishes the thought of winning the contest or displaying one's skill in technique, swordsmanship is doomed.

TAKANO SHIGIYOSHI

The sort of man who, throwing a stone upon the ground, would miss.

IDRIES SHAH

The fortitude to make failure the yardstick of achievement, and the sanity to discern that the greatness of art is its unimportance.

ALBERTO GIACOMETTI

Treat success and failure as the twin imposters they are.

RUDYARD KIPLING

Give me a fruitful error any time, full of seeds, bursting with its own corrections. You can keep your sterile truths for yourself.

VILFREDO PARETO

Man is air in the air and in order to become a point in the air he has to fall.

ANTONIO PORCHIA

The idea of winning absolutely is abhorrent to people who must depend on each other for the harvest. Take wrestling. In the West, we pin. In African wrestling, the loser is merely thrown off balance. And the loser dances out.

ROBERT THOMPSON

Last night as I lay sleeping I dreamt that there was a beehive here inside my heart and the golden bees were making white combs and sweet honey from all my failures.

MACHADO DE ASSIS

FAKES

This is either a forgery or a damn clever original!

FRANK SULLIVAN

An art dealer (this story is authentic) bought a canvas signed "Picasso" and traveled all the way to Cannes to discover whether it was genuine. Picasso was working in his studio. He cast a single look at the canvas and said; "It's a fake." A few months later the dealer bought another canvas signed "Picasso." Again he traveled to Cannes and again Picasso, after a single glance, grunted: It's a fake." "But cher maitre," expostulated the dealer, "it so happens that I saw you with my own eyes working on this picture several years ago." Picasso shrugged: "I often paint fakes."

ARTHUR KOESTLER

It took me a long time to discover that the key thing in acting is honesty. Once you know how to fake that, you've got it made.

ACTOR IN PEYTON PLACE

One of the Second Republic's most grandiose ideas had been to establish a Museum of Copies in Paris, which would reproduce the best paintings of the whole world, and in 1851 four painters were dispatched to copy the works in the National Gallery in London.

THEODORE ZELDIN

A 20th-Century Fox executive in Paris arranged for an exhibit of the fake paintings used in the movie How To Steal A Million. He phoned Howard Newman of the New York office who said the fakes could not be shipped because they were on tour. "What should I do?" asked the Paris man frantically. "Get some originals," said Newman. Nobody'll know the difference."

Working with Hitchcock early in her career actress Ingrid Bergman was uncomfortable about the way he had asked her to play a certain scene. "I don't think I can do that naturally," she told him and went on to explain her difficulties and suggest possible alternatives. Hitchcock listened solemnly, nodding from time to time; Miss Bergman felt she had made her case. "All right," he finally said, "If you can't do it naturally, then fake it."

CLIFTON FADIMAN

Even Vermeer – that miraculous breathless stillness. Even the sunlight in Vermeer has a magical fraudulence. What is magic after all but an inspired and lovely fraudulence?

FREDERIC PROKOSCH

I have calculated that if I see a film that lasts an hour, I am in fact plunged into absolute blackness for twenty minutes. In making a film, I am thus guilty of fraud.

INGMAR BERGMAN

FAREWELL/PARTING

Be ahead of all parting, as though it already were behind you.

RAINER MARIA RILKE

The last blackbird lights up his gold wings: farewell.

Of all the things I do, parting is the inevitable one.

YEHUDA AMICHAI

My name is Might-have-been; I am also called No-more, Too-late, Farewell.

DANTE GABRIEL ROSSETTI

Some day when I lose you, will you still be able to sleep, without me to whisper over you like a crown of linden branches?

RAINER MARIA RILKE

There is no conclusion. There are no fortunes to be told, and no advice to be given. Farewell.

BUCKMINSTER FULLER

FEAR

Remember how easy it was, being afraid? – you look back and yearn for the distance of terror, how aesthetic fear was. These fluttering hands now press hard fingerprints onto a freezing face, and suddenly you know why it moves, why you feel it so well. It is yours.

WILLIAM STAFFORD

One has to fear everything – or nothing.

JEAN GIRAUDOUX

Mankind owns four things that are no good at sea: rudder. anchor, oars – and the fear of going down.

ANTONIO MACHADO

Who is more foolish, the child afraid of the dark or the man afraid of the light?

MAURICE FREEHILL

One must not look inward too much, while the inside is yet tender, I do not wish to frighten myself until I can stand it.

DJUNA BARNES

George (in Tom Stoppard's Jumpers) cites the Greek philosopher Zeno, who concluded that "since an arrow shot towards a target first had to cover half the distance, and then half the remainder, and then half the remainder after that and so on ad infinitum, the result was... that though an arrow is always approaching its target, it never quite gets there, and Saint Sebastian died of fright."

You see, one thing is, I can live with doubt and uncertainty and not knowing. I think it's much more interesting to live not knowing than to have answers which might be wrong. I have approximate answers and possible beliefs and different degrees of certainty about different things, but I'm not absolutely sure of anything and there are many things I don't know anything about, such as whether it means anything to ask why we're here... I don't have to know an answer. I don't feel frightened by not knowing things, by being lost in a mysterious universe without any purpose, which is the way it really is as far as I can tell. It doesn't frighten me.

RICHARD FEYNMAN

Just as a man shudders with horror when he thinks he has trodden on a serpent, but laughs when he stoops and sees that it is only a rope, so I discovered one day that what I was calling "I" is not apparent, and all fear and anxiety vanished with my mistake.

GAUTAMA

You always become the thing you fight the most.

CARL JUNG

FREEDOM

Freedom of will is the ability to do gladly that which I must do.

CARL JUNG

BREATHING ON YOUR OWN

If you think you're free, there's no escape possible.

BABA RAM DASS

To find yourself you need the greatest possible freedom to drift.

FRANCIS BACON

To hold, you must first open your hand. Let go.

TAO TE CHING

If you want something very very badly, let it go free. If it comes back to you, it's yours forever. If it doesn't, it was never yours to begin with.

I don't know if I am free because I am unhappy or unhappy because I am free.

JEAN-LUC GODARD

Freedom is what you do with what's been done to you.

JEAN-PAUL SARTRE

Purpose? Man can only hope for "the will be make oneself completely free - Will is the wrong word, because in the end you would call it despair. Because it really comes out of an absolute feeling of it's impossible to do these things, so I might as well just do anything. And out of this anything one sees what happens."

FRANCIS BACON

I have discovered a country where the pages of books are all margins.

RICHARD SHELTON

GOD

The wave can never be afraid of the ocean.

SULTAN VELAD

Lily Tomlin as Sister Boogie Woman: "People say to me, 'Sister, I don't believe in nothin! I believe it's all done with mirrors.' Boogie is believin' in the maker of those mirrors."

If only God would give me some clear sign. Like making a large deposit in my name at a Swiss bank.

WOODY ALLEN

Dear God, your book has a lot of zip to it. I like science-fiction stories. Your reader, Jimmy

Slipping on my shoes, boiling water, toasting bread, buttering the sky: that should be enough contact with God in one day to make anyone crazy.

HAFIZ

The physicist Leo Szilard once announced to his friend Hans Bethe that he was thinking of keeping a diary: "I don't intend to publish it; I am merely going to record the facts for the information of God." "Don't you think God knows the facts?" Bethe asked. "Yes," said Szilard. "He knows the facts, but he does not know this version of the facts."

What will you do, God, when I die?

RAINER MARIA RILKE

You are the deep innerness of all things. The last word that can never be spoken. To each of us you reveal yourself differently: to the ship as a coastline, to the shore as a ship.

RAINER MARIA RILKE

God says to the soul, "I am the noise of water, rain coming. You are so thirsty. How can you fall asleep?"

RUMI

And once when saying his prayers, which he (Sydney Smith) always did out loud, he was overheard to say: "Now lord, I'll tell you an anecdote."

PATRICK MAHONY

If I have learned one thing in this life, it is that God will not tie my shoes without me.

DOUG BOYD

I wonder how God lives in heaven, when the clouds seem to be collapsing like broken birds.

JEWELL LAWTON, AGE 8

Here's the new rule: break the wineglass, and fall towards the glassblower's breath.

RUMI

If you don't make yourself equal to God you can't perceive God: for like is known by like.

THE HERMETIC WRITINGS, 3RD CENTURY

HAPPINESS

The terror is all promises are kept. Even happiness.

Keep knocking, and the joy inside will eventually open a window and look out to see who's there.

RUMI

And now I have to confess the unpardonable and the scandalous. I am a happy man. And I am going to tell you the secret of my happiness. It is quite simple. I love mankind. I love love. I hate hate. I try to understand and accept.

JEAN COCTEAU

What would there be in a story of happiness? Only what prepares it, only what destroys it can be told.

ANDRÉ GIDE

We are happy when for everything inside us there is a corresponding something outside us.

W.B. YEATS

You'd get the boss on the line and say, "Listen, I've been sick ever since I started working here, but today I'm well and I won't be in anymore." Call in well.

TOM ROBBINS

Happy people have no right to be optimists; it is an insult to sorrow.

JULES RENARD

Be happy. It's one way of being wise.

COLETTE

And the sun and moon sometimes argue over who will tuck me in at night. If you think I am having more fun than anyone on this planet you are absolutely correct.

HAFIZ

Perhaps all pleasure is only relief.

WILLIAM BURROUGHS

Happiness is a question of changing your troubles.

COLETTE

There is no pleasure in having nothing to do; the fun is in having lots to do and not doing it.

JOHN W. RAPER

Won't you come into the garden? I would like my roses to see you.

RICHARD B. SHERIDAN

In order to be utterly happy the only thing necessary is to refrain from comparing this moment with other moments in the past, which I often did not fully enjoy because I was comparing them with other moments of the future.

ANDRÉ GIDE

If you want an hour's happiness, get drunk. If you want three days' happiness, take a wife. If you want three month's happiness, kill a pig and eat it for three months. But if you want to be happy all your life, be a gardener.

CHINESE PROVERB

She is such a good friend that she would throw all her acquaintances into the water for the pleasure of fishing them out.

TALLEYRAND

Ah, if only we knew how to blossom: our heart would pass beyond every small danger, and would find peace in the greatest danger of all.

RAINER MARIA RILKE

Happiness is not an elusive bird, perched high near the ceiling, which, with the help of more or less complicated ladders, you have to work to catch. Happiness is an element, which, like air, is everywhere.

JACQUES HENRI LARTIGUE

HEART

The heart is an infinity of massive chains, chaining little handfuls of air.

ANTONIO PORCHIA

Heart, I told you before and twice, and three times, don't knock at that door. No one will answer.

ANONYMOUS SPANISH FOLK SONG

The poet's heart, like all other hearts, is an interminable artichoke.

PABLO NERUDA

Above all do not plant me in your heart. I grow much too fast.

Dr. Adrian Kantrowitz feels that many times it will not be necessary to remove the whole heart in a transplant operation. "We can leave it at least for sentimental value," he said.

NEWSPAPER

And that heart which was a wild garden was given to him who loved only trim lawns. And the imbecile carried the princess into slavery.

ANTOINE DE SAINT-EXUPERY

You have what is called thin skin: if I put my ear to it I can hear the wingbeat in your heart. I can only imagine how far down those flights go.

PLUMLY

My heart is like a flame turned upside down.

GUILLAUME APOLLINAIRE

The greatest explorer on this earth never takes voyages as long as those of the man who descends to the depth of his heart.

JULIEN GREEN

Hippocrates had no means of recognizing the heart as a pump, because there was no such item in his world, and no such word in his vocabulary.

GUIDO MAJNO, M.D.

Now you must go out into your heart as onto a vast plain. Now the immense loneliness begins.

RAINER MARIA RILKE

Perhaps our heart is made of the answer that is never given.

RENÉ CHAR

I carefully number the bricks of my heart for a later reconstruction.

JEFF SILVA

The work of the eye is complete now; work next at the heart's work – on those images you've captured within you, led in and overcome and left unknown. Look inside bridegroom – on your inside bride, so superbly drawn out of a thousand natures: a beauty thus far won, but thus far never loved.

RAINER MARIA RILKE

I don't know who it is who lives or dies, who rests or wakes, but it is your heart that distributes all the graces of the daybreak in my breast.

PABLO NERUDA

HOPE

Says yes when nobody asked.

LAO PROVERB

The basis of optimism is sheer terror.

OSCAR WILDE

You watched them sewing you up – hope with his needle and thread – knowing that all you really needed of yourself was the part they would not let you keep.

RICHARD SHELTON

And somebody would come and knock on this air long after I have gone and there in front of me a life would open.

W.S. MERWIN

Erv had a gift for optimism. He believed what he wanted to. Ruth said that if Erv tossed a ball in the air three times, tried to hit it three times with a bat, and three times missed, he would, undisturbed, conclude: Wow, what a pitcher.

STEVE FISHMAN

Flowers are without hope. Because hope is tomorrow and flowers have no tomorrow.

ANTONIO PORCHIA

In the garden I plant my hands – I know I shall grow, I know, I know – swallows will lay their eggs in the nest of my inkstained fingers.

FORUGH FARROKHZAD

I dwell in Possibility.

EMILY DICKINSON

I imagine that yes is the only living thing.

E.E. CUMMINGS

My business is Circumference.

EMILY DICKINSON

I shall be a dawn made of all the air I ever breathed.

SAINT GERAUD

Twice I have lived forever in a smile.

E.E. CUMMINGS

HUMAN NATURE

She was doing her laundry. She turned to me and said... you know, I love this machine much more than I do your Uncle Walter.

JOHN CAGE

My neighbor Howard says his mother saved everything. His mother made little cloth bags to hold pieces of string, each bag carefully labeled as to the length of the pieces. After her death they found one small bag of string labeled "too short to save."

BEVINGTON

"How do you teach – is the world round or flat?" The teacher looked for some hint of the desired answer. Finding none, he finally said: "I can teach it either way."

NEWSPAPER

There is the wire Chesterton sent to his wife while away from home to deliver a lecture in a town in the Midlands: "Am in Market Harborough. Where ought I to be?"

Man with wooden leg escapes prison. He's caught. They take his wooden leg away from him. Each day he must cross a large hill and swim a wide river to get to the field where he must work all day on one leg. This goes on for a year. At the Christmas Party they give him back his leg. Now he doesn't want it. His escape is all planned. It requires only one leg.

JAMES TATE

I refuse to admit I'm more than 52, even if that does make my sons illegitimate.

LADY ASTOR

When at any time there is a blundering or confusion in a maneuver, roll in amongst the soldiers and lay about you from right to left. This will convince people that it is not your fault.

FRANCIS GROSE ADVICE TO OFFICERS. 1762

But I mark my beginning as a professional biographer from the day when my bank bounced a check because it was inadvertently dated 1772.

R. HOLMES

The famous French soldier Marshall Lyautey asked his gardener to plant a row of trees of a certain rare variety in his garden the next morning. The gardener said he would be glad to do so, but he cautioned the Marshall that trees of this size take a century to grow to full size. "In that case," replied Lyautey, "plant them this afternoon."

DOUGLAS HOFSTADER

B. M. (Victoria Sackville-West) had once papered a room at Knole entirely with used postage stamps.

I have read that the Rev. C. R. Maturin (the author of Gothic novels), when in the throes of composition, used to be seen with a red wafer stuck on his forehead, a sign to his numerous family that he was not to be spoken to.

FREDERICK LOCKER-LAMPSON

Two villagers decided to go bird hunting. They packed their guns and set out with their dog into the fields. Near evening, with no success at all, one said to the other, "We must be doing something wrong." "Yes," agreed the friend, "perhaps we're not throwing the dog high enough."

ANONYMOUS JOKE BY WAY OF MARVIN MINSKY

My daughter once asked me if I was alive when the world was black and white, because everything she saw that was old on TV was black and white.

CHUCK CLOSE

I always find that statistics are hard to swallow and impossible to digest. The only one I can ever remember is that if all the people who go to sleep in church were laid end to end they would be a lot more comfortable.

MRS. ROBERT A. TAFT

BREATHING ON YOUR OWN

General Richard S. Ewell, who fought gallantly for the Confederacy at Winchester and Gettysburg sometimes halluci-nated that he was a bird. For hours at a time he would sit in his tent softly chirping to himself, and at mealtimes he would accept only sunflower seeds or a few grains of wheat.

About Julia Margaret Cameron – Victorian photographer: The night before the poet Henry Taylor visited the Cameron house, on the Isle of Wight, Julia decided that the guest room was too dark for such a luminary to stay in, so she engaged carpenters to work all night adding a west window in time for the sunshine to be pouring in at the poet's arrival the next afternoon.

HELMUT GERNSHEIM

He just kept saying he'd always wanted to drive. (Buffalo police officer Karen Czekalski, on a blind man who drove for three miles before ramming into a telephone pole).

NEWSWEEK

Wittgenstein writes about a man who, not being certain of an item he reads in the newspaper, buys 100 copies of the paper to reassure himself of its truth.

HUMOR

Chronic schizophrenic, when asked at what age he began to coin words, replied: "Age 20, when I developed a sense of humor."

DAVID FORREST

You find out that the universe is a system that creeps up on itself and says "Boo!" and then laughs at itself for jumping.

ALAN WATTS

In the words of a Chinese Zen master: "Nothing is left to you at this moment but to have a good laugh!"

I am ashamed of my century for being so entertaining but I have to smile.

FRANK O'HARA

What I want is to make people laugh so they'll see things seriously.

WILLIAM ZINSSER

But humor can't go hand in hand with revolution. Humor means multiple viewpoints, which revisionists cannot afford.

NED ROREM

As soon as you have made a thought, laugh at it.

LAO TZU

Like all young men I set out to be a genius, but mercifully laughter intervened.

LAWRENCE DURRELL

Analyzing humor is like dissecting a frog. Few people are interested and the frog dies of it.

E.B. WHITE

IDEAS

An idea isn't responsible for the people who believe in it.

DON MARQUIS

Everyone is a genius at least once a year. The real geniuses simply have their bright ideas closer together.

GEORGE LICHTENBERG

When desire is silenced and the will comes to rest, the world-as-idea becomes manifest.

I CHING

One is not likely to doubt that 2 plus 2 equals 4 until one begins to think more carefully about the objects to which this theorem applies. It is empirically true for fingers, apples, and all other objects whose identity does not change in the process of counting. But what about clouds in the sky, which merge and separate as the wind propels them? Do two ideas plus two ideas always make four ideas?

I don't have any ideas that are more than seven hundred words long.

A COLUMNIST

Kierkegaard noticed that the less support an idea has, the more fervently it must be believed in, so that a totally preposterous idea requires absolute unflinching faith.

I do not know anything about completeness in love, except the idea I have of it.

COLETTE

And what if the idea of punishment preceded, not followed wrongdoing?

BEREL LANG

To die for an idea is to place a pretty high price upon conjecture.

ANATOLE FRANCE

IMAGINATION

Our imagination is stretched to the utmost, not, as in fiction, to imagine things which are not really there, but just to comprehend those things which are there.

RICHARD FEYNMAN

Don't wait till you die to see this. Recognize that your imagination and your thinking and your sense-perception are reed canes that children cut and pretend are horsies.

RUMI

To return what exists to pure possibility; that is the deep, the hidden work.

PAUL VALERY

If you have an imagination that goes far afield, you can live far afield.

PATRICIA HIGHSMITH

In dreams, in memory, as in the sense of sight, our imagination is the organizing force of our life, of our world. Each man, in his turn, must reinvent the things around him.

ROBBE-GRILLET

What I demand is accuracy for the sake of imagination.

EUGÉNE DELACROIX

Nothing is ever the same as they said it was. It's what I've never seen before that I recognize.

DIANE ARBUS

IMITATION/THEFT

Originality is undetected plagiarism.

WILLIAM INGE

Copy from one, it's plagiarism; copy from two, it's research.

WILSON MIZNER

The immature poet imitates; the mature poet plagiarizes.

T.S. ELIOT

BREATHING ON YOUR OWN

Nicholas Murray Butler and Professor Branden Matthews of Columbia University were having a conversation and Professor Matthews was giving his ideas as to plagiarism, from an article of his own on that subject. "In the case of the first man to use an anecdote," he said, "there is originality; in the case of the second, there is plagiarism; with the third, it is lack of originality; and with the fourth, it is drawing from a common stock." "Yes," broke in President Butler, "and in the case of the fifth, it is research."

B.A. BOTKIN

Originality is nothing but judicious imitation.

FRANÇOIS VOLTAIRE

I imitate everyone except myself.

PABLO PICASSO

The difference between a bad artist and a good one is: The bad artist seems to copy a great deal; the good one really does.

WILLIAM BLAKE

In any art you're allowed to steal anything if you can make it better.

ERNEST HEMINGWAY

If there's something to be stolen, I steal it.

PABLO PICASSO

IMPORTANCE

I do not pin the least butterfly of life on importance.

ANDRÉ BRETON

It is the end of importance.

JILL JOHNSTON

BREATHING ON YOUR OWN

I have no point of view.

JOHN CAGE

There is no ultimate reason for calling anything important or valuable; no ultimate reason for preferring one thing to another.

JOHN BARTH

Every person, every event is equally worth watching. Choice and selection, the distinctions of the artist, are tyrannous and deluding.

JEAN-LUC GODARD

Everything exists. Nothing has value.

E. M. FORSTER

Kill it at once or let it go.

W.S. MERWIN

From the Persian monarch who, having to adjudicate upon two poems, caused the one to be read to him, and at once, without ado, awarded the prize to the other.

SIR ARTHUR QUILLER-COUCH

I think it is because everything, from the explosion of a nova to the fall of dust in a deserted room, is of vast and equal significance, and therefore meaningless.

JOHN BANVILLE

To be able to listen – without presupposing, classifying, improving, controverting, evaluating, approving or disapproving, without dueling what is being said... such listening is rare.

ABRAHAM MASLOW

That's what it finally comes down to; to see everything, all elements equal, in life; even the mystical, even death. No one thing may extend beyond the other and each must rein its neighbor in.

RAINER MARIA RILKE

The necessary and the unnecessary are the same because they both eliminate the need for value judgments.

JASPER JOHNS

IN BETWEEN

Keep attentive between the two breaths. Forget breaths. Keep attentive in between. Breathe the intangible breath – the invisible part of breath.

RAJNEESH

Sit very quietly, and when the scenery shifts, slip between it.

We are not committed to this or that. We are committed to the nothing in-between... whether we know it or not.

JOHN CAGE

And you are left, to no one belonging wholly, not so dark as a silent house, nor quite so surely pledged unto eternity as that which grows and climbs the night.

RAINIER MARIA RILKE

I don't paint things. I only paint the difference between things.

HENRI MATISSE

When I was in India I met and conversed briefly with Shri Atmananda Guru of Trivandrum: and the question he gave me to consider was this: "Where are you between two thoughts?"

JOSEPH CAMPBELL

The essence of film is in the interval.

DZIGA VERTOV

I have made a great discovery. I no longer believe in anything. It is not the object that matters to me but what is between them: it is this "in-between" that is the real subject of my pictures.

GEORGE BRAQUE

There is something very odd about all of this. That which you cannot put your finger on, that which always escapes you, that which is completely elusive – the blank – seems to be absolutely necessary for there to be anything whatsoever.

ALAN WATTS

INDIVIDUALITY

If the wind means me, I'm here! Here.

THEODORE ROETHKE

Close your hand – do you feel an absence or a presence?

BRENDA HEFTY

The question of where we are going is of course extremely important; but equally important, it seems to me, is the question of who is going.

CARL JUNG

Can't see? Steal your own things.

KOREAN PROVERB

People who have their feet planted firmly on the ground often have difficulty getting their pants off.

My poverty is not complete. It lacks me.

ANTONIO PORCHIA

Be a lamp, or a lifeboat, or a ladder.

RUMI

BREATHING ON YOUR OWN

I learn from the land. Some day like a field I may take the next thing so well that whatever is will be me.

WILLIAM STAFFORD

You refuse to own yourself, you permit others to do it for you.

MARGARET ATWOOD

I am the razor that has been put away, also the wrist in the photograph, and – lately – also the photographer.

JEAN VALENTINE

"If no man is an island," cried Morris Irving Hyman, "I'm the narrowest peninsula in the world."

V. PORCHE

We are what we imagine. Our very existence consists in our imagination of ourselves... the greatest tragedy that can befall us is to go unimagined.

N. SCOTT MOMADAY

We are what we pretend to be, so we must be careful about what we pretend to be.

KURT VONNEGUT, JR.

Yes, I will try to be. Because I believe that not being is arrogant.

ANTONIO PORCHIA

All the information I have about myself is from forged documents.

VLADIMIR NABOKOV

Our job is to become more and more of what we are. I have said elsewhere that the growth of a poet sometimes seems to me to be related to his or her becoming less and less embarrassed about more and more.

MARVIN BELL

There are in me the seeds from which, if necessary, the universe could be reconstructed. In me somewhere there is a matrix for mankind and a holograph for the whole world. Nothing is more important in my life than trying to discover these secrets.

TED SIMON

They will say you are on the wrong road, if it is your own.

ANTONIO PORCHIA

Ecstasy is the final stage of intimacy with yourself.

RUMI

It was when I was living with my cousins that I suddenly woke up to the fact that if I accepted anybody's definition of what there was in the world, I would be limited.

SHIRLEY BRICE HEATH

Well, you've got to stand for something or you'll fall for anything.

COUNTRY WESTERN SONG

El Tornillo walks the streets of Melo. People in town think he's crazy. He carries a mirror in his hand and he looks at himself with furrowed brow. He doesn't take his eyes off the mirror. "What are you doing, Tornillo?" "I'm here," he says, "keeping watch on the enemy."

EDUARDO GALEANO

Messages from the universe arrive addressed no more specifically than "To Whom It May Concern."

NORBERT WIENER

He might be waiting for an ambulance, a naked woman, or the Seraphim of God. But he's not. He's going to get up and paint his room at midnight with himself in the corner saying, "This is myself. This is the bed. This is the plastic cup. I am one, I am welcome, like the chair, the table, any of the objects there."

LEONARD COHEN

Everyone is indispensable.

JEAN RENOIR

Lend yourself to others, but give yourself to yourself.

MICHEL DE MONTAIGNE

If you want to hold the beautiful one, hold yourself to yourself.

RUMI

All of us invent ourselves. Some of us just have more imagination than others.

CHER

If I had not created my whole world, I would certainly have died in other people's.

ANAIS NIN

Include the knower in the known.

JULIAN JAYNES

Who can tell the dancer from the dance?

W.B. YEATS

A Judge sits. A defendant stands: may I always work standing.

JEAN COCTEAU

If I don't manage to fly, someone else will. The spirit wants only that there be flying. As for who happens to do it, in that he has only a passing interest.

RAINER MARIA RILKE

INEVITABILITY

Simply trust. Do not the petals flutter down, just like that?

ISSA

Your duty is to be; and not to be this or that.

RAMANA MAHARSHI

The apple tree is a very complicated thing. But for the apple tree it is easy.

INDIAN HOLY MAN

Learn to wish that everything should come to pass exactly as it does.

EPICTETUS

Everything should be as simple as it is, but not simpler.

ALBERT EINSTEIN

No snowflake ever falls in the wrong place.

ZEN PROVERB

INNOCENT EYE

Monet once said that he wished he had been born blind and later gained sight. That way he would be able to look at the world freed of the knowledge of what the objects were so that he could more fully appreciate their color.

An aquarium maintains creatures from another world; it's like a reverse submarine.

JAMES GORMAN

What if your knees bent the other way, what would a chair look like?

"Is it on?"

THREE-YEAR-OLD BOY HOLDING BALL-POINT PEN.

"A pier," Stephen said, "Yes, a disappointed bridge."

JAMES JOYCE

I am trying to be unfamiliar with what I'm doing.

JOHN CAGE

Each act is virgin, even the repeated one.

RENÉ CHAR

Astronomy is biased toward things that glow in the dark.

After watching many planes fly over her home, a child was boarding a plane for the first time. Turning to her mother, she whispered, "When do we get smaller?"

If there were no dust, housekeeping would be an art form.

JOHN THORNE

"You certainly have a lovely baby." "That's nothing. You should see his photograph."

The greatest masterpiece in literature is only a dictionary out of order.

JEAN COCTEAU

The Gothic cathedrals were meant to be seen. They remained in the villages that built them, there to inspire religious awe in generations to come. So too with the pyramids, which have survived for millennia. SAS-1, however was built to be thrown away. Once declared perfect, it would never be seen again — it would be launched, briefly used, and then burned up upon re-entry when its orbit degraded several years later. A strange intent for such a work of art.

GEORGE GREENSTEIN

I'm in a phone booth at the corner of Walk and Don't Walk.

"Daddy, are we live or on tape?"

Jono Abel was the son of the well-known U.S. actor Walter Abel. At age seven he had never seen a play, although he had watched his father in films. The first time his mother, Marietta, took him to the theater to see his father, he cried out in astonishment, "Look, Mom! Round actors!"

CLIFTON FADIMAN

INVISIBLE

For such is our task: to impress this fragile and transient earth so sufferingly, so passionately upon our hearts that its essence shall rise up again, invisible, in us. We are the bees of the invisible… The Elegies show us engaged in this work, the work of the perpetual transformation of beloved and tangible things into the invisible vibration and excitability of our nature, which introduces new "frequencies" into the fields of the universe.

RAINER MARIA RILKE

Tell me what you see vanishing and I will tell you who you are.

W.S. MERWIN

Dream of the transparent children, the light in them. I love transparence.

ANAIS NIN

Buckminster Fuller was right when he claimed that ninety-nine percent of reality was invisible.

Whose idea was this, to have the lover visible and the Beloved invisible! So many people have died of their desiring because of this. The lover cannot kiss the lips he wants, so he bites himself!

RUMI

Earth, isn't this what you want – invisibly to arise in us? Is it not your dream to be someday invisible?

RAINER MARIA RILKE

BREATHING ON YOUR OWN

All that is visible around us is in itself inexpressible, whereas what's expressible is within us, in itself, invisible.

AVIGDOR ARIKHA

The trouble with you, Robert, is that you make the visible world too easy to see.

ATTRIBUTED TO WALLACE STEVENS, AFTER ROBERT FROST HAD
ALLEGEDLY COMPLAINED ABOUT THE OBSCURITY OF STEVENS' POEMS

"Hafiz, is it true that our destiny is to turn into Light itself?" And I replied, "Dear moon, now that your love is maturing, we need to sit together close like this more often."

HAFIZ

Vision is the art of seeing things invisible.

JONATHAN SWIFT

My obligation is this: To be transparent.

PABLO NERUDA

The fact is, I still work attempting to be invisible. Often, I have to start off attempting to do something by slipping into another con-sciousness that allows me to be the spectator while I'm working, so that there's at least an audience of one. And sometimes that can be a crowd.

ROBERT RAUSCHENBERG

You shoot to find yourself, I shoot to disappear.

ALEJANDRO JODOROWSKY

KISSES

A paper bird in my breast says that the time for kisses hasn't come.

VINCENTE ALEXANDRE

I close your ear with kisses and seal your nostrils, and round your neck you'll wear – nay, let me work – a delicate chain of kisses. Like beads they go around and not one misses to touch its fellow on either side.

D.H. LAWRENCE

Kisses belong to the shadows, but they shine in the night like stars.

RÉMY DE GOURMONT

As the adjective is lost in the sentence, so I am lost in your eyes, ears, nose, and throat – you have enchanted me with a single kiss which can never be undone until the destruction of language.

KENNETH KOCH

A kiss is like singing into someone's mouth.

DIANE ACKERMAN

'Tis a secret, Told to the mouth instead of to the ear.

EDMOND ROSTAND

"Stay," he said, his right arm around her waist and her face expectantly turned to him, "shall it be the kiss pathetic, sympathetic, graphic, paragraphic, Oriental, intellectual, paroxysmal, quick and dismal, slow and unctuous, long and tedious, devotional, or what?" She said perhaps that would be the better way.

CHARLES BOUSBAUGH

I would love to kiss you. The price of kissing is your life. Now my love is running toward my life shouting, what a bargain, let's buy it.

RUMI

LANGUAGE

Language is a virus from outer space.

LAURIE ANDERSON AND WILLIAM BURROUGHS

There is absolutely no chance for a word to express anything. As soon as we start putting our thoughts into words and sentences, everything goes wrong.

MARCEL DUCHAMP

We never arrive at fundamental propositions in the course of our investigation; we get to the boundary of language which stops us from asking further questions. We don't get to the bottom of things, but reach a point where we can go no further, where we cannot ask further questions.

LUDWIG WITTGENSTEIN

How describe the delicate thing that happens when a brilliant insect alights on a flower? Words, with their weight, fall upon the picture like birds of prey.

JULES RENARD

I always tell a young man not to use the word "always".

ROBERT WALPOLE

Since the concepts people live by are derived only from perceptions and from language and since the perceptions are received and interpreted only in light of earlier concepts, man comes pretty close to living in a house that language built.

RUSSELL. W. SMITH

Each language performs an artificial chopping up of the continuous flow of existence in a different way. Children repattern every day. Mississippi is not Mrs. Sippy, the equator is not a menagerie lion but an imaginary line.

ADAM SMITH

The great thing about human language is that it prevents us from sticking to the matter at hand.

LEWIS THOMAS

The limits of my language mean the limits of my world.

LUDWIG WITTGENSTEIN

The word "water" is itself undrinkable, and the formula H_2O will not float a ship.

ALAN WATTS

"Then you should say what you mean," the March Hare went on. "I do," Alice hastily replied. "At least – at least I mean what I say – that's the same thing you know." "Not the same thing a bit!" said the Hatter. "Why, you might just as well say that 'I see what I eat' is the same thing as 'I eat what I see.' "

LEWIS CARROLL

The poem is supposed to be endless, because the moment I write about the tiger, the tiger isn't the tiger, he becomes a set of words in the poem.

JORGE LUIS BORGES

A language is a map of our failures.

ADRIENNE RICH

What can't be said can't be said and it can't be whistled either.

RAM TIRTHA

The difference between the right word and the almost right word is the difference between lightning and the lightning bug.

MARK TWAIN

Our words misunderstand us.

ADRIENNE RICH

Our language, or any language based so heavily on nouns, has a Tinkertoy structure. To get beyond it would take a language like that of the Nootka, which is all verbs (to refer to a table one says "it tables"). In altered states of consciousness I sometimes experience the world in this verbal form – a totality expressing itself in ways for varying periods of time: tabling, flowering, flooring, kittening, grassing, pavementing.

PHILIP SLATER

"Therefore" is a word the poet must not know.

ANDRÉ GIDE

The fish trap exists because of the fish. Once you've gotten the fish you can forget the trap. The rabbit snare exists because of the rabbit. Once you've gotten the rabbit, you can forget the snare. Words exist because of meaning. Once you've gotten the meaning, you can forget the words. Where can I find a man who has forgotten words so I can talk with him?

CHUANG TZU

Our alphabet's first sound is but the lengthening of a sigh.

JOSEPH BRODSKY

The paradox of culture is that language, the system most fre- quently used to describe culture, is by nature poorly adapted to this difficult task. It is too linear, not comprehensive enough, too slow, too limited, too constrained, too unnatural, too much a product of its own evolution, and too artificial.

EDWARD HALL

I distrust all words, I have reached the point, alas, of comparing those words on which we so lightly traverse the space of a thought, to light planks thrown across an abyss, which permit crossing but no stopping. A man in quick motion can use them and get away; but if he hesitates the least bit in the world, this fraction of time breaks them down, and all together fall into the depths.

PAUL VALERY

In the spectrum there are no boundaries: each language can divide it into as many, or as few, sections as it chooses. When it was first realized that some of our shades of color were absent from the Homeric epics, it was suggested that Homer must have been color blind.

STEPHEN ULLMANN

Words do not signify anything but their own reality. Therefore it is important to keep changing the subject.

JOHN BROCKMAN

LEARNING

Personally I'm always ready to learn, although I do not always like being taught.

WINSTON CHURCHILL

When I read a book on Einstein's physics of which I understood nothing, it doesn't matter: that will make me understand something else.

PABLO PICASSO

My green thumb came only as a result of the mistakes I made while learning to see things from the plant's point of view.

H. FRED ALE

To correct: to arrange surprise.

BUCKMINSTER FULLER

The little I know, I owe to my ignorance.

SACHA GUITRY

The next message you need is always right where you are.

RAM DASS

The failure to understand the significance of play in maturing human beings has had incalculable consequences, because play is not only crucial to learning but (unlike other drives) is its own reward.

EDWARD HALL

One should say "expiration," not "inspiration." It is from our reserves, from our night that things come to us, our work pre-exists within us. The problem is to discover it. We are merely its archaeologists.

They always told me when I was young, "Just wait, and you'll see." Now I'm old and see nothing. It's wonderful.

ERIC SATIE

I used to be a design but now I'm a tree.

8 YR. OLD

You have to know how far to go too far.

JEAN COCTEAU

I know nothing. Learn of me.

W.S. MERWIN

Perhaps my life is nothing but an image of this kind: perhaps I am doomed to retrace my steps under the illusion that I am exploring, doomed to try and learn what I should simply recognize, learning a mere fraction of what I have forgotten.

ANDRÉ BRETON

There's a kind of waiting you teach us — the art of not knowing.

WILLIAM STAFFORD

The important thing is not so much that every child should be taught, as that every child should be given the wish to learn.

JOHN LUBBOCK

Process is our most important product. Points of view are beside the point.

JOHN BROCKMAN

We are in a crises where we are finding that the old systems don't work. But that sort of disillusionment is only discovering that what you thought was so, isn't. It's the first step in learning. So I celebrate disillusionment.

BUCKMINSTER FULLER

We learn nothing from the things we know.

JOHN CAGE

The best thing for being sad, replied Merlyn, beginning to puff and blow, is to learn something. You may grow old and trembling in your anatomies, you may lie awake at night listening to the disorder of your veins, you may miss your only love, you may see the world about you devastated by evil lunatics, or know your honor trampled in the sewers of baser minds. There is only one thing for it then – to learn.

T.H. WHITE

If a little knowledge is dangerous, where is the man who knows so much as to be out of danger.

THOMAS HUXLEY

Every parent should also remember the existence of so-called backward learning, that undressing comes before dressing, emptying boxes is achieved long before they are ever filled, and a mess is made – repeatedly – before anything is tidied up. Much of learning proceeds from trial to error and only belatedly to success. We must first fall off our bicycles, and much of learning is achieved by being given the opportunity to fail.

ANTHONY SMITH

The question is how immediately are you going to say yes to no matter what unpredictability.

JOHN CAGE

All that I've learned, I've forgotten. The little that I still know, I've guessed.

CHAMFORT

BREATHING ON YOUR OWN

Dr. Kasner had two main audiences: the great mathematicians of two continents and children. I think he slightly preferred the children. It was his theory that the way to interest children in mathematics was to begin with difficult concepts and gradually work up to the multiplication table. It was a sound theory. His own nine-year-old nephew was so apt a student of higher mathematics that he invented a number. (about Edward Kasner 1878-1955 – Adrian Chair in Mathematics at Columbia University.)

CLIFTON FADIMAN

Andres Segovia once said his interest in the guitar began when he was 8 years old. "One day a man walked by me in the street playing a guitar. He put my fingers on the strings and I played, not as if I were learning but as if I was remembering."

LIFE

Life is too important a thing ever to talk seriously about it.

OSCAR WILDE

Life is a handkerchief sandwich.

JOHN BERRYMAN

I say to my breath once again, little breath come from in front of me, go away behind me, row me quietly now, as far as you can, for I am an abyss that I am trying to cross.

W.S. MERWIN

I don't want to live life the way I see it. I'll play my life by ear.

16 YEAR OLD

You are always in the beginning of some prophecy that you will not believe to save your life.

JAY WRIGHT

So you're the kind of vegetarian that only eats roses.

LEONARD COHEN

Granted, we die for good. Life, then is largely a thing of happens to like, not should.

WALLACE STEVENS

Often he would hold his hand over the flame of a candle to persuade himself that he was alive. Since his death he keeps beside him a lit candle but hides his hands.

JULES SUPERVIELLE

Pasternak says life creates incidents to divert our attention from it so that it can get on with the work it can only accomplish unobserved.

Again the cry that it's late and the islands are just beginning to rise.

W.S. MERWIN

If you give what can be taken, you are not really giving. Take what you are given, not what you want to be given. Give what cannot be taken.

INDRIES SHAH

The mystery of life is not a problem to be solved but a reality to be experienced.

AART VAN DER LEEUW

The whole work of a man really seems to consist in nothing but proving to himself every minute that he is a man and not a piano key.

FEODOR DOSTOYEVSKY

Computers are always right, but life isn't about being right.

JOHN CAGE

Plans, marriages and journeys appear to me just as foolish as if someone falling out a window were to hope to make friends with the occupants of the room before which he passes.

JEAN COCTEAU

BREATHING ON YOUR OWN

Artists have at least a form within which they can hold their own conflicting opposites together. But there are some who have no recognized artistic form to serve this purpose. They are artists of living. To my mind, these last are the supreme heroes in our soulless society.

IRENE CLAREMONT DE CASTILLEJO

You've got to outlast yourself.

CLINT EASTWOOD

To be a poet of life, though artists seldom realize it, is the summum. To breathe out more than one breathes in.

HENRY MILLER

Life must go on; I forget just why.

EDNA ST. VINCENT MILLAY

How very much of one piece is what befalls us, in what a relationship one thing stands to another, has given birth to itself and grows up and is brought up to itself, and we in reality have only to exist, but simply, but ardently, as the earth exists, assenting to the years, light and dark and altogether in space, not desiring to be at rest in anything save in the net of influences and forces in which the stars feel themselves secure.

RAINER MARIA RILKE

The universe isn't run on the point system. And survival isn't what it's all about. Do what you're going to do; and with humor be aware that you might as well be doing the opposite.

R.K. WELSH

We who lived in concentration camps can remember the men who walked through the huts comforting others, giving away their last piece of bread. They may have been few in number, but they offer sufficient proof that everything can be taken from a man but one thing: the last of the human freedoms – to choose one's attitude in any given set of circumstances, to choose one's own way.

VICTOR FRANKEL

We are traveling with tremendous speed toward a star in the Milky Way. A great repose is visible on the face of the earth. My heart's a little fast. Otherwise everything is fine.

BERTOLT BRECHT

Yes, Dr. Miller says we are pessimistic because life seems like a very bad, very screwed up film. If you ask "What the hell is wrong with the projector?" and go up to the control room, you find it's empty. You are the projectionist, and you should have been up there all the time.

COLIN WILSON

Everyone is in the best seat.

JOHN CAGE

It is much more sensible to be an optimist instead of a pessimist, for if one is doomed to disappointment, why experience it in advance?

AMELIA PEABODY EMERSON

He combined skepticism of everything with credulity about everything; and I am convinced this is the true Shakespearean way wherewith to take life.

JOHN COWPER POWYS

The things by which we live are the distant flashes of insect wings.

RAYMOND CHANDLER

The soul moves in circles, said Plotinus. Hence our lives are not moving straight ahead; instead, hovering, wavering, returning, renewing, repeating.

JAMES HILLMAN

Since our vision is so limited, let's go!

RUMI

BREATHING ON YOUR OWN

No one can make you feel inferior without your consent.

ELEANOR ROOSEVELT

When asked what he was, Duchamp said, he was a "respirateur," a breather.

The art of living is the art of knowing how to believe lies.

CESARE PAVESE

Look. This is your world! You can't not look. There is no other world. This is your world; it is your feast. You inherited this; you inherited these eyeballs; you inherited this world of color. Look at the greatness of the whole thing. Look! Don't hesitate. Open your eyes. Don't blink.

CHOGYAM TRUNGPA

You know the rule: If you are falling, dive. Do the thing that has to be done.

JOSEPH CAMPBELL

For there is no place that does not see you. You must change your life.

RAINER MARIA RILKE

Take your life in your own hands and what happens? A terrible thing. No one to blame.

ERICA JONG

The only sensible way to regard life is that it is a privilege you are willing to pay for.

ROBERT HENRI

Suzuki Roshi once said about questioning our life, our purpose – "It's like putting a horse on top of a horse and then climbing on and trying to ride. Riding a horse is hard enough. Why add another horse? Then it's impossible."

For me the artist simply means one who can transform ordinary life into a beautiful creation, with his craft. But I did not mean creation strictly applied only to the arts. I meant creation in life, the creation of a child, a garden, a house, a dress. I was referring to creativity in all its aspects. Not only the actual products of art, but the faculty for healing, consoling, raising the level of life, transforming it by our own efforts.

ANAIS NIN

How goes a life? Something like the ocean building dead coral.

STANLEY MOSS

Yes, I will try to be. Because I believe that not being is arrogant.

ANTONIO PORCHIA

If you want to know the taste of a pear, you must change the pear by eating it yourself.

MAO TSE TUNG

Do unto others as they wish, but with imagination.

MARCEL DUCHAMP

Life must be understood backwards. But it must be lived forwards.

SÖREN KIERKEGAARD

We are asleep with compasses in our hands.

W.S. MERWIN

My grandfather always said that living is like licking honey off a thorn.

LOUIS ADAMIC

Sit, walk, or run, but don't wobble.

ZEN

BREATHING ON YOUR OWN

We die at the age of forty from a bullet that we shot into our heart at twenty.

ALBERT CAMUS

As Anita Loos said, "Fate keeps on happening."

Live by the foma (harmless untruths) that make you brave and kind and healthy and happy.

KURT VONNEGUT, JR.

My own beliefs are unbelievable.

JOHN LILLY

To succeed consider what is as though it were past. Deem yourself inevitable and take credit for it. If you find you no longer believe, enlarge the temple.

W.S. MERWIN

LOCKS/KEYS

You think I'm speaking these words? When a key turns in a lock, the lock makes a little opening sound.

RUMI

Standing still, I can hear my footsteps come up behind me and go on ahead of me and come up behind me and with different keys clinking in the pockets, and still I do not move.

W.S. MERWIN

The more I approach you in reality, the more the key sings in the door of the unknown room.

ANDRÉ BRETON

The small man builds cages for everyone he knows. While the sage, who has to duck his head when the moon is low, keeps dropping keys all night for the beautiful rowdy prisoners.

HAFIZ

LOGIC

You are not thinking. You are merely being logical.

NIELS BOHR TO ALBERT EINSTEIN

A story should have a beginning, a middle, and an end... but not necessarily in that order.

JEAN-LUC GODARD

The wisest thing to do is to open one's ears immediately and hear a sound suddenly before one's thinking has a chance to turn it into something logical, abstract, or symbolical.

JOHN CAGE

The Austrian-born philosopher Ludwig Wittgenstein once remarked that if you ask a man how much is 2 plus 2 and he tells you 5, that is a mistake. But if you ask a man how much is 2 plus 2 and he tells you 97, that is no longer a mistake. The man you are talking with is operating with a wholly different logic from your own.

THOMAS FRIEDMAN

Pure logical thinking cannot yield us any knowledge of the empirical world; all knowledge of reality starts from experience and ends in it. Propositions arrived at by purely logical means are completely empty of reality.

ALBERT EINSTEIN

In the main, and from the beginning of time, mysticism has kept men sane; the thing that has driven them mad is logic.

G. K. CHESTERTON

The thing that astonished him was that cats should have two holes cut in their coat exactly at the place where their eyes are.

G.C. LICHTENBERG

A mind all logic is like a knife all blade. It makes the hand bleed that uses it.

RABINDRANATH TAGORE

Two parallel lines meet somewhere in infinity, and they believe it.

G.C. LICHTENBERG

LOSS

And if you still find something, you have not lost everything. You still have to lose something.

ANTONIO PORCHIA

We are led one thing at a time through gain to that pure gain – all that we lose.

WILLIAM STAFFORD

Yes, I will go. I would rather grieve over your absence than over you.

ANTONIO PORCHIA

Sighs are air, and go to the air, tears are water, and go to the sea. Tell me fair one, if you know: when love is forgotten, where can it go?

GUSTAVO ADOLFO BECQUER

Memory is the only kind of loss we ever know.

RICHARD SHELTON

Your absence has gone through me like thread through a needle. Everything I do is stitched with its color.

W.S. MERWIN

And I fell through all your absent arms with the star I had never flung desperately back to weld apart my heart.

SAINT GERAUD

LOST/FOUND

If you have any notion of where you are going, you will never get anywhere.

JOAN MIRO

Because we have lost whoever they are calling, we say that they are not calling us.

W.S. MERWIN

The things of mine that are utterly lost are the ones that, when I lost them, were not found by someone else.

ANTONIO PORCHIA

The first step... shall be to lose the way.

GALWAY KINNELL

The poet does not keep what he discovers; having transcribed it, soon loses it. Therein lies his novelty, his infinity, and his peril.

RENÉ CHAR

Lost with all hands is an old story.

LAWRENCE RAAB

The best thing we can do is make wherever we're lost look as much like home as we can.

FRY

Most police departments recognize the claim that any man who wants to get lost has the right to do so.

NEWSPAPER

"Where you headed from here?" "I don't know." "Can't get lost then." conversation in Nameless, Tennessee

WILLIAM LEAST HEAT MOON

The American artist Chester Harding, painting Daniel Boone's portrait, asked the old frontiersman, then in his eighties, if he had ever been lost. Boone replied "No, I can't say I was ever lost, but I was bewildered once for three days."

I am for the art of things lost.

CLAES OLDENBURG

All the fish needs is to get lost in water.

CHUANG TZU

The day in the woods I took a compass was the day I got lost for sure.

JOHN CAGE

Until we lose ourselves there is no hope of finding ourselves.

HENRY MILLER

LOVE

Love is much nicer to be in than an automobile accident, a tight girdle, a higher tax bracket or a holding pattern over Philadelphia.

JUDITH VIORST

Being a woman, you will say when you put this letter down "Well, he can't love me very much, as he would have made more fuss." Good God! More fuss when my heart feels like a peche Melba.

HAROLD NICOLSON, LETTER TO VITA SACKVILLE-WEST

Have all of the keys removed from your typewriter except the ones needed to spell her name.

It's a love story. No one's ahead.

Love is an act of endless forgiveness, a tender look which becomes a habit.

PETER USTINOV

He thought that she must have a lovely, an exquisitely beautiful skeleton. She would lie in the ground like a piece of matchless lace, a work of art in ivory, and in a hundred years might be dug up and turn the heads of old archaeologists. Every bone was in place, as finely finished as a violin... Boris imagined that he might be very happy with her, that he might even fall in love with her, could he have her in her beautiful bones alone... Many human relations, he thought, would be infinitely easier if they could be carried out in the bones only.

ISAK DINESEN

Hello, last page of my life...

CHEKHOV IN 1899 LETTER TO OLGA KNIPPU, WHOM HE LATER MARRIED, FOUR YEARS BEFORE HIS DEATH.

What is irritating about love is that it is a crime that requires an accomplice.

CHARLES BAUDELAIRE

When someone asks what it means to "die for love," point here.

RUMI

All these words are just a front. What I would really like to do is chain you to my body, then sing for days and days and days.

HAFIZ

The old Duc de Broglie, reminiscing in company about memorable letters he had received, recalled, "The one that gave me the greatest satisfaction was one I got from a very lovely lady. It consisted of only one word." "And that was?" said one of the guests. "Friday."

W. SCHOLZ

Or as some French author – De Maupassant, I believe – said: "The best part of love is walking up the stairs."

HENRY MILLER

Any time that is not spent on love is wasted.

TASSO

Oh, there's so many. Can I give you just one that I really like? It was from a little boy. He sent me a charming card with a little drawing. I loved it. I answer all my children's letters – sometimes very hastily – but this one I lingered over. I sent him a postcard and I drew a picture of a Wild Thing on it. I wrote "Dear Jim, I loved your card." Then I got a letter back from his mother and she said, "Jim loved your card so much he ate it." That to me was one of the highest compliments I've ever received. He didn't care that it was an original drawing or anything. He saw it, he loved it, he ate it.

MAURICE SENDAK

A million light years and a million more would not give time enough to store that small second of eternity when I took you in my arms and you took me in yours.

JACQUES PREVERT

Have you forgotten that you are my page for this day?

RAINER MARIA RILKE

"Which foolish man was it who said love was simple?" she murmured, "Ah, yes it was Rodolphe. But which Rodolphe?"

LEON GARFIELD

Farewell, but you will be with me, you will go within a drop of blood circulating in my veins or outside, a kiss that burns my face or a belt of fire at my waist. My sweet, accept the great love that came out of my life and that in you found no territory like the explorer lost in the isles of bread and honey.

PABLO NERUDA

You don't know nights of love? Don't petals of soft words float upon your blood? Are there no places on your dear body that keep remembering eyes?

RAINER MARIA RILKE

Just give me a little more time! I want to love the things as no one has thought to love them, until they're real and ripe and worthy of you.

RAINER MARIA RILKE

Your hands closed on my chest and there like two wings they ended their journey.

PABLO NERUDA

All my life I have longed to be loved by a woman who was melancholy, thin, and an actress. Now I have been, and I am not happy.

MARIE-HENRI STENDHAL

We do what only lovers can... make a gift out of necessity.

LEONARD COHEN

He claims for his newly freed hero only a willingness to "settle for the stamina of love, a presence he felt like the beginnings of a stair."

JOHN CHEEVER

Madame, people very seldom die because they lost someone. I believe they die more often because they haven't had someone.

COLETTE

If I had had a pistol I would have shot him – either that or fallen at his feet. There is no middle way when one loves.

LADY TROUBRIDGE

You began to be irreplaceable for me long before I had ever heard of you.

ROGER SALE

Waiting to take up again the duty of the one who loves best: the daily imposture, the deferential lie, the passionately maintained dupery, the unrecognized feat of valor that expects no reward....

COLETTE

You fall in love by suddenly knowing what past love hadn't.

JOHN FOWLES

"Why must one always potter around in a garden? Can't you potter around in an armchair as well?" "I did once," confessed Snubbers moodily... "Gad, sir, what a wildcat she was!" He chewed his wad of carbon paper reminiscently.

S.J. PERELMAN

Love is in many ways at its best when it is born doomed. Passion without the future of home and fidelity plucks the roses a little more desperately while it may. Its sky is full of fiddles and its days leap about like a ballet dancer. Its impermanence gives it not only an extra life but an extra dimension. In such a love, one postures, invents, acts, and thus the dimension of art is added to kisses. It is a muddle head and a liar who kisses, but also an artist. He creates for himself and sometimes for his bewildered lover a beauty beyond truth and reality.

BEN HECHT

Return to the most human, nothing less will teach the angry spirit, the bewildered heart, the torn mind, to accept the whole of its duress, and pierced with anguish, at last act for love.

MAY SARTON

Love's not a potato. You can't throw it out the window.

RUSSIAN PROVERB

Out of this great beast springs Prince Charming. And the Prince asks: "Are you happy?" And Beauty replies: "I shall have to get used to it."

JEAN COCTEAU

I know well enough that this image – fixed forever in my mind is not you, but the shadow of love which exists in me... and although I know this, I then think that without you, without the rare excuse you gave me, my love, now a tenderness today would be there within sleeping still and lying in hope... then I thank you.

LUIS CERNUDA

Nothing is more vain than to die for love. What we ought to do is live.

ALBERT CAMUS

The night before last night I heard that to make songs to girls and to make prayers to god were of equal value in the eye of time; provided, that is, that the prayers are sufficiently beautiful.

BURMESE

Between no place of mine and no place of yours, you'd have thought I'd know the way by now.

W.S. MERWIN

I am the least difficult of men. All I want is boundless love.

FRANK O'HARA

Even stones have a love, a love that seeks the ground.

MAESTER ECKHART

A love which cannot bear to be faced with reality is not a real love. But then, it is the privilege of noble hearts not to be able to love.

ALBERT CAMUS

Read my lips, forget my name.

WILLIAM STAFFORD

Her clothes have no buttons. There are two missing from my jacket. This lady and I are almost of the same religion.

GUILLAUME APOLLINAIRE

Everything is relevant. I call it loving.

JAMES TATE

A printer brooding on the loss of the woman he loved, set her name in type and swallowed it.

One must have teeth. Then love's like biting into an orange when the juice squirts in your teeth.

BERTOLT BRECHT

I love you as you are, but do not tell me how that is.

ANTONIO PORCHIA

And someone you love enters the room and says wouldn't you like the eggs a little different today? And when they arrive they are just plain scrambled eggs and the warm weather is holding.

FRANK O'HARA

Are not all lovers forever wounding the margins of each other in their pursuit of freedom, of pursuit, of home? So in a moment's intuition a base of paradox appears in pain that we may see; and all is clear to us.

RAINER MARIA RILKE

I would die of your fingers if I could be buried in your palm.

MALAY SAYING

It is easier to enter heaven than to pass through each other's eyes.

SAINT GERAUD

I am gathering poppies from the dangerous fields of your eyebrows.

OSSIP MANDELSTAM

The art of love? It's knowing how to join the temperament of a vampire to the discretion of an anemone.

E.M. CIORAN

I'm going to make you think about me every minute of the day. I put a picture of you behind the door and I stuck two pins in your eyes. Now you're going to think about me for the rest of your life because the pins have fallen out of the picture.

GABRIEL GARCIA MARQUEZ

Is night more easy on lovers? Ah, they only hide their fate from themselves by using each other. Don't you know that yet? Throw the emptiness from your arms into the spaces we breathe, so maybe the birds can feel the expanded air more ardently flying.

RAINER MARIA RILKE

MAPS

Geographers in the Soviet Union face an unusual occupational hazard. For reasons which must have something to do with national security, no published map of the USSR published in the Soviet Union can be accurate. Each river, city and town must be moved slightly from its actual location.

ROBERT KAISER

An ideal map would contain the map of the map, the map of the map of the map … endlessly.

ALFRED KORZYBSKI

My grandfather told me once that the best map is one that points to which way is north and shows you how much water is in your way.

STEPHEN KING

Hold the map close to your face. Breathe into it and you will hear a river start.

GREG KUZMA

The Pole of Relative Inaccessibility is "that imaginary point on the Arctic Ocean farthest from land in any direction." It is a navigator's paper point contrived to console Arctic explorers who, after Peary and Henson reached the North Pole in 1909, had nowhere special to go.

ANNIE DILLARD

Burn all the maps to your body.

RICHARD BRAUTIGAN

"That's another thing we've learned from your nation," said Mein Herr, "map-making. But we've carried it much further than you. What do you consider the largest map that would be really useful?" "About six inches to the mile." "Only six inches!" exclaimed Mein Herr. "We very soon got to six yards to the mile. Then we tried a hundred yards to the mile. And then came the grandest scale of a mile to the mile!" "Have you used it much?" I inquired. "It has never been spread out, yet!" said Mein Herr: "the farmers objected: they said it would cover the whole country, and shut out the sunlight! So we now use the country itself, as its own map, and I assure you it does nearly as well."

LEWIS CARROLL

MEANING

The only true thoughts are those which do not grasp their own meaning.

PABLO NERUDA

Everything that man has handled has a tendency to secrete meaning.

MARCEL DUCHAMP

How is it possible to find meaning in a finite world, given my waist and shirt size?

WOODY ALLEN

Life is so meaningless we might as well try to make ourselves extraordinary.

FRANCIS BACON

There it is. I don't believe in anything, but I'm always glad to wake up in the morning. It doesn't depress me. I'm never depressed. My basic nervous system is filled with this optimism. It's mad, I know, because it's optimism about nothing. I think of life as meaningless and yet it excites me. I always think something marvelous is about to happen.

FRANCIS BACON

As for the meaning of life, I do not believe that it has any. I do not ask what it is, but I suspect it has none and this is a source of great comfort to me. We make of it what we can and that is all there is about it.

ISAIAH BERLIN

When you have grasped its meaning with your will, then tenderly your eyes will let it go.

RANIER MARIA RILKE

The situation reached the height of the ludicrous when I suddenly realized one day that of everything I had written about the man I could just as well have said the opposite. I had indubitably reached that dead end which lies so artfully hidden in the phrase "the meaning of meaning."

HENRY MILLER

Why say what is? Why afflict the things with their meaning? I can imagine only a longing that with continual wandering traverses the world.

RAINER MARIA RILKE

Mean something! You and I, mean something! Ah, that's a good one!

SAMUEL BECKETT

MEASURING

A measurement measures measuring means.

JOHN CAGE

The strongest proof of Wittgenstein's relentlessness with regard to precise measurements is perhaps the fact that he decided to have the ceiling of a hall-like room raised by three centimeters just as the cleaning of the completed house was to commence.

ANTHONY STORR

If you liberate yourself from the measurement of time, you can't continue to take structure completely seriously.

JOHN CAGE

Jung-kwang asks, "How much does this glass of water weigh?" Puzzled, I reply, "I don't know. Half a pound or so." He slaps his hand on the table and laughs. "Are you still measuring?"

MEMORY

"I'm sure (my memory) only works one way;" Alice remarked. "I can't remember things before they happen." "It's a poor sort of memory that only works backwards," the Queen remarked.

LEWIS CARROLL

Can you remember what remembering was like last Tuesday?

LUDWIG WITTGENSTEIN

I've got a good memory for forgetting.

ROBERT LOUIS STEVENSON

Why should we suppose that what we remember is more important than what we forget?

DORIS LESSING

Alifano: But why is time ungraspable? Borges: Undoubtedly, because time is made up of memory. And that memory is made up largely of forgetfulness.

What we remember can be changed. What we forget we are always.

RICHARD SHELTON

I was always an avid forgetter: in my two human hands only the untouchable things of the world live unscathed.

PABLO NERUDA

Men live by forgetting – women live on memories.

T.S. ELIOT

In 1802 Kant discharged Lampe, the faithful servant who had been with him for years. But he could not dismiss him from his mind; this began to trouble him greatly. He therefore made an entry in his memorandum book: "Remember, from now on the name of Lampe must be completely forgotten."

IMMANUEL KANT

When I was younger I could remember anything, whether it had happened or not.

MARK TWAIN

What can a flame remember? If it remembers a little less than is necessary, it goes out; if it remembers a little more than is necessary, it goes out. If only it could teach us, while it burns, to remember correctly.

GEORGE SEFERIS

BREATHING ON YOUR OWN

But when from a long-distant past nothing subsists, after the people are dead, after the things are broken and scattered, taste
and smell alone, more fragile but more enduring, more insub-
stantial, more persistent, more faithful, remain poised a long
time, like souls, remembering, waiting, hoping, amid the ruins of
all the rest; and bear unflinchingly, in the tiny and almost impal-
pable drop of their essence, the vast structure of recollection.

MARCEL PROUST

Smoke. Remember who lets you go.

W.S. MERWIN

One of the oddest things in life, I think, is the thing one remembers.

AGATHA CHRISTIE

For example, they have made the paradoxical discovery that forgetting serves a very important function, and is a by-product of
learning. Computers are now being programmed to forget selec-
tively, as the brain does, rather than store every item of information in its memory.

JOSEPH CAMPBELL

I think that if I recall something, for example, if today I look back
on this morning, then I get an image of what I saw this morning.
But if tonight, I'm thinking back on this morning, then what I'm
really recalling is not the first image, but the first image in memory. So that every time I recall something, I'm not recalling it really, I'm recalling the last time I recalled it. I'm recalling my last
memory of it. So that really, I have no memories whatever. I have
no images whatever, about my childhood, about my youth.

JORGE LUIS BORGES

Quite literally, a man's memory is what he forgets with.

The same wind that tells you everything at once unstitches your
memory. You try to write faster than the thread is pulled.

W.S. MERWIN

And it is not yet enough to have memories. You must be able to forget them when they are many, and you must have the immense patience to wait until they return. For the memories themselves are not important. Only when they have changed into our very blood, into glance and gesture, and are nameless, no longer to be distinguished from ourselves – only then can it happen that in some very rare hour the first word of a poem arises in their midst and goes forth from them.

RAINER MARIA RILKE

One has not understood Zen until one has forgotten it.

DAISETZ SUZUKI

Things stored up by memory for forgetfulness.

JORGE LUIS BORGES

I pause in my game to consider the loveliest of my days. But I let them be. There are periods of life that are too precious for reliving. Rapture – the union of dream and fulfillment – I would rather not pry among such past events. In fact – I avoid remembering them as much as I can, putting them out of my thought, gently, when they reappear. This is not because their memory would sadden me, but because to remember past joys is somehow to misuse them. They were not meant for memory to fondle. That I still smile, hope, and love is a better proof (and use) of their existence.

BEN HECHT

I am writing the memoirs of a man who has lost his memory.

EUGENE IONESCO

You cannot compare this present experience with a past experience. You can only compare it with a memory of the past, which is a part of the present experience.

ALAN WATTS

Not a leaf in the forest survives our recall.

PABLO NERUDA

Where are our great forgetters – who will teach us to forget about such and such a part of the world – where is the Christopher Columbus to whom once again we will owe the forgetting of an entire vast continent of creation – to lose – but to lose truly – to make room for discovery.

GUILLAUME APOLLINAIRE

Tu Fu served in the office of "Reminder" at the emperor's court.

MEN/WOMEN

"How wonderful women are," says a character in one of Sacha Guitry's plays. "How tender and sympathetic they are, how they minister to us when we are ill." Then, almost as an afterthought, "But we can't always be ill, can we?"

It occurred to me when I was 13 and wearing white gloves and Mary Janes and going to dancing school, that no one should have to dance backwards all their lives.

JILL RUCKELSHAUS

Jonathan Swift, himself the author of an important essay on meaning, left behind him at his death this note, attached to a lock of his secret love Stella's hair: "only a woman's hair."

If all your bones were candles, your face would still be a dark answer.

SAINT GERAUD

You breathe in carbon dioxide and exhale oxygen.

ANTOINE ARTAUD

A woman must have a pretext in giving herself to a man. What better than to appear to be yielding to force?

DE LACLOS

"When one of us dies, I'll move to the Riviera," said a woman to her husband when she saw the beautiful Mediterranean coast.

As for me, I've come to take you for the muse of my off-days.

JAMES MERRILL

A woman tries to comfort me. She puts her hand under my shirt and writes the names of flowers on my back.

MARK STRAND

When someone admired a nightgown she had bought in Paris, Djuna Barnes said, "Yes, I spent all summer looking for a night to go with that nightgown."

"I've got ground glass in my bones," she said.

GABRIEL MARQUEZ

Her hearing was keener than his, and she heard silences he was unaware of.

D.M. THOMAS

I asked Margot if she thought I was very ugly. She said that I was quite attractive and that I had nice eyes. Rather vague, don't you think?

ANNE FRANK

Where would you keep her? What with the great, strange thoughts in your head coursing in and out, and mostly staying the night?

RAINER MARIA RILKE

How can a woman be expected to be happy with a man who insists on treating her as if she were a perfectly normal human being.

OSCAR WILDE

"When may I come and visit you?" asked Marcel. "I'll paint your portrait." "My dear, I can give you no address, since perhaps tomorrow I shall have none. But I'll come to see you, and I'll mend your coat, which has a hole in it so big that you could move all your furniture through it without paying any rent." "What a sweet girl," said Marcel, as he walked slowly away, "a very goddess of gaiety. I'll make two holes in my coat."

HENRI MURGER

Women never have young minds. They are born three thousand years old.

SHELAGH DELANEY

I would venture to guess that Anon., who wrote so many poems without signing them, was often a woman.

VIRGINIA WOOLF

A beautiful woman who is pleasing to men is good only for frightening fish when she falls into the water.

ZEN

A man is privileged when his passion obliges him to betray his convictions to please the woman he loves.

RENÉ MAGRITTE

If you were this poem I would not be its writer.

SAINT GERAUD

Sometimes to someone lonely there comes something that works as a wondrous balm. It is not a sound, not even a voice. It is the smile of women – a smile, that, like the light of perished stars, is still on its way.

RAINER MARIA RILKE

Women have a much better time than men in this world: there are far more things forbidden them.

OSCAR WILDE

Your eyes. It's a day's work just looking into them.

LAURIE ANDERSON

Your little boat has no anchor and my little boat has no sail.

We, in the struggling nights, keep falling from nearness to nearness; where the woman in love is dew, we are a plummeting stone.

RAINER MARIA RILKE

Just think – tonight, tonight, when the moon is sneaking around the clouds, I'll be sneaking around you. I'll meet you tonight under the moon. Oh, I can see you now – you and the moon. You wear a necktie, so I'll know you.

GROUCHO MARX TO MARGARET DUMONT

Next to the wound, what women make best is the bandage.

JULES BARBEY D'AUREVILLY

"Madox, what is the name of that hollow at the base of a woman's neck? At the front. Here. What is it, does it have an official name? That hollow about the size of an impress of your thumb?" Madox watches me for a moment through the noon glare. "Pull yourself together," he mutters.

MICHAEL ONDAATJE

What I had to go through to make that man a sculptor!

MABEL DODGE LUHAN

Women who can only give all or nothing don't know the meaning of pleasure.

COLETTE

MENTAL ILLNESS

Nobody realizes that some people expend tremendous energy merely to be normal.

ALBERT CAMUS

I could have been a marvelous madman. I could have contained my madness.

HENRI LANGLOIS

The point is, if there were only one person in the world, it would be impossible for that person to be insane.

ROBERT PIRSIG

I have lived on the lip of insanity, wanting to know the reasons, knocking on a door. It opens. I've been knocking from the inside!

RUMI

Sanity is the most profound moral option of our time.

RENATA ADLER

Some people never go crazy. What truly horrible lives they must live.

CHARLES BUKOWSKI

What do you think would happen to you if you systematically copied the body language of a schizophrenic?

MORRIS BERMAN

When dealing with the insane, the best method is to pretend to be sane.

HERMAN HESSE

I have never seen a more lucid, more lonely, better balanced mad mind than mine.

VLADIMIR NABOKOV

The most common last straw leading to admission to mental hospitals in the United States in 1972 was – what would you think? – smashing the television set.

ROSS SPECK

A psychotic is a guy who's just found out what's going on.

WILLIAM BURROUGHS

Ask not what disease the person has, but rather what person the disease has.

WILLIAM OSLER

MIND

Two monks were arguing about the temple flag. One said the flag moved, the other said the wind moved. Master Eno overheard them and said, "It is neither the wind nor the flag, but your mind that moves."

My mind has been in control all of my life and it would kill me rather than relinquish control.

CARLOS CASTENADA

Trying to please the brain is like trying to drink through your ears.

I would suggest (as an exercise) that sometime you take your two eyes along with you – and leave your intellect and your friends intellects at home – you might without these handicaps begin to see things – that would surprise you.

JOHN MARIN

The mind cannot possibly repeat itself.

PAUL VALERY

BREATHING ON YOUR OWN

It requires a very unusual mind to undertake the analysis of the obvious.

ALFRED NORTH WHITEHEAD

James Jenkins believes that we remember experiences which have a personal meaning for us, even if the meaning is a pure construction of the mind. "I think we will eventually conclude that the mind remembers what the mind does, not what the world does."

I must have a prodigious quantity of mind; it takes me as much as a week sometimes to make it up.

MARK TWAIN

Whenever we read a book or have a conversation, the experience causes physical changes in your brain. In a matter of seconds, new circuits are formed, memories that can change forever the way you think about the world. It's a little frightening to think that every time you walk away from an encounter, your brain has been altered, sometimes permanently.

GEORGE JOHNSON

Mind is everything. Mind pulls the universe out of a top hat, bows to its own applause, and walks off the stage, grinning.

STEPHEN MITCHELL

I've given up on my brain. I've torn the cloth to shreds and thrown it away.

RUMI

Physics is the study of the structure of consciousness. The stuff of the world is mindstuff.

SIR ARTHUR EDDINGTON

Since we are destined to live out our lives in the prison of our minds, our one duty is to furnish it well.

PETER USTINOV

For the brain, there is no illusion. There is no line making arbitrary divisions such as good and bad, normal and perverse, sanity and insanity. Reality is whatever the brain is doing.

JOHN BROCKMAN

MIRRORS

We are two mirrors crossing their swords.

OCTAVIO PAZ

The world is the mirror of myself dying.

HENRY MILLER

The abandonment of all disguises, the marriage of the mirrors.

HENRI COULETTE

A mirror dreams only of another mirror....

ANNA AKHMATOVA

To stay young, to save the world, break the mirror.

NANAO SAKEKI

"The empty mirror," he said. "If you could really understand that, there would be nothing left here for you to look for."

ZEN

If you are irritated by every rub, how will your mirror be polished?

RUMI

Mirrors would do well to think before they cast their reflections back at us.

JEAN COCTEAU

Man's mind is a mirror of a universe that mirrors man's mind.

JOSEPH PEARCE

He steps into the mirror, refusing to be anyone else.

FRANK O'HARA

MISTAKES

I'll figure out as best I can what I ought not to do and then do it. If I don't make any mistakes who will believe my errors? I'll change my whole person and then when I'm different and no one can recognize me I'll keep doing the same things that I did since I couldn't possibly do otherwise.

PABLO NERUDA

I have woven a parachute out of everything broken.

WILLIAM STAFFORD

If I wanted to be consistent, I would have stayed home.

The best thing in Dada was – "God can afford to make mistakes. So can Dada!"

HENRY MILLER

The best way to learn is by your own mistakes. The people who write textbooks do not make mistakes.

14 YR. OLD

Fred Astaire once said to Jack Lemmon, "You're at a level where you can only afford one mistake. The higher up you go, the more mistakes you're allowed. Right at the top, if you make enough of them, it's considered to be your style."

QUENTIN CRISP

A sea which is a mistake is impossible.

ODYSSEUS ELYTIS

We are built to make mistakes, coded for error.

LEWIS THOMAS

If you don't make mistakes you're not working on hard enough problems. And that's a big mistake.

F. WILEZEK

Do you ever make silly mistakes? It's one of my very few creative activities.

LEN DEIGHTON

Every decision you make is a mistake.

EDWARD DAHLBERG

MOTIVATION

Inside my empty bottle I was constructing a lighthouse while all the others were making ships.

CHARLES SIMIC

It takes no more energy to write fortissimo than to write piano, universe than garden.

PAUL VALERY

There is no reason why a kaleidoscope should not have as much fun as a telescope.

MARK TWAIN

Being a somewhat dark person myself, I fell in love with the idea that what you look for your whole life will eventually eat you alive.

LAURIE ANDERSON

The highest purpose is to have no purpose at all.

JOHN CAGE

Matisse once told the Hollywood film star Edward G. Robinson that the only thing that drove him to paint was the rising urge to strangle someone.

Be careful where you aim. You might get there.

CHET ATKINS

I write when I cannot not write.

JEAN COCTEAU

Now that the moon is out of a job, it has an easy climb.

WILLIAM STAFFORD

Do everything. One thing may turn out right.

HUMPHREY BOGART

MUSIC

I never practice. I always play.

WANDA LANDOWSKA

Virtuoso pianist Lorin Hollander recalls: "By the time I was three, I was spending every waking moment at the keyboard, standing, placing my hands on the keyboard and pushing notes. And I would choose very carefully what tones I would choose because I knew that when I would play a note I would become that note."

The composer Stravinsky had written a new piece with a difficult violin passage. After it had been in rehearsal for several weeks, the solo violinist came to Stravinsky and said he was sorry, the passage was too difficult, no violinist could play it. Stravinsky said, "I understand that. What I am after is the sound of someone trying to play it."

THOMAS POWERS

In the late 1600s the finest instruments originated from three rural families whose workshops were side by side in the Italian village of Cremona. First were the Amatis, and outside their shop hung a sign: "The best violins in all Italy." Not to be out-done, their next door neighbors the family Guarnerius, hung a bolder sign proclaiming: "The Best Violins In All The World!." At the end of the street was the workshop of Anton Stradivarius, and on its front door was a simple notice which read: "The best violins on the block."

FREDA BRIGHT

The Indians long ago knew that music was going on permanently and that hearing it was like looking out a window at a landscape which didn't stop when one turned away.

JOHN CAGE

I remembered a story of how Bach was approached by a young admirer one day and asked, "But Papa Bach, how do you manage to think of all these new tunes?" "My dear fellow," Bach is said to have answered, according to my version, "I have no need to think of them. I have the greatest difficulty not to step on them when I get out of bed in the morning and start moving around my room."

LAURENS VAN DER POST

A little girl, after hearing Beethoven's Ninth Symphony for the first time, asked, "What do we do now?"

Remember, the music is not in the piano.

CLEMENT MOK

I love Beethoven, especially the poems.

RINGO STARR

Reminds me of a passage in one of Schumann's piano sonatas marked, "As fast as possible," which is followed a few bars later with the admonition, "Faster."

From the New York State Journal of Medicine comes this report: In Rome, surgeon Gaetano Zappalo has been using Bach fugues to treat indigestion. Mozart is ideal for rheumatism, Handel for broken hearts and other disturbed emotional states, Beethoven for hernia and Schubert for insomnia.

The meaning of music lies not in the fact that it is too vague for words, but that it is too precise for words.

FELIX MENDELSSOHN

Mozart said: "I have never made the slightest effort to compose anything original."

MYSTERY

The most beautiful thing we can experience is the mysterious. It is the source of all true art and science. He to whom the emotion is a stranger, who can no longer pause and stand wrapped in awe, is as good as dead; his eyes are closed.

ALBERT EINSTEIN

Enchantment is destroyed by vagueness and mystery exists only in precise things.

JEAN COCTEAU

If one looks at a thing with the intentions of trying to discover what it means, one ends up no longer seeing the thing itself, but thinking of the question that has been raised. One cannot speak about mystery; one must be seized by it.

RENÉ MAGRITTE

It was something to do with the sound... the way sound made images, shell within shell of them softly unclosing... the way words became colors and scents... and the surprise when it happened, the ache of desire, the surge of excitement, the sense of fulfillment, the momentary perception of something unknowable....

ROSAMOND LEHMANN

There is a mystery in all great writing and that mystery does not dissect out. It continues and it is always valid. Each time you re-read you see or learn something new.

ERNEST HEMINGWAY

In the palm of one hand now the rain falls. From the other the grass grows. What can I tell you.

VASKO POPA

The only valid thing in art is the one thing that cannot be explained. To explain away the mystery of a great painting would do irreplaceable harm, for whenever you explain or define something you substitute the explanation or the definition for the image of the thing.

HENRI MATISSE

By and large it is an inborn tendency of mine to deal with the secret as such, not as something to be unmasked but as the mystery which remains mystery right to its core, the secret which is all secret just as a lump of sugar is sugar through and through.

RAINER MARIA RILKE

They gave him a sea shell: "So you'll learn to love the water." They opened a cage and let a bird go free: "So you'll learn to love the air." They gave him a geranium: "So you'll learn to love the earth." And they gave him a little bottle sealed up tight. "Don't ever, ever open it. So you'll learn to love mystery."

EDUARDO GALEANO

No object is mysterious. The mystery is your eye.

ELIZABETH BOWEN

In a letter to Henri Moudor who had sent her a black lead drawing of a rose, Colette wrote: "I am looking at it through my magnifying glass, and thank God, I can discover nothing, you have left it all its mystery."

It is important to have a secret, a premonition of things unknown. It fills life with something impersonal, a numinosum. A man who has never experienced that has missed something important. He must sense that he lives in a world which in some respects is mysterious. That things happen and can be experienced which remain inexplicable; that not everything which happens can be anticipated. The unexpected and incredible belong in this world. Only then is life whole.

CARL JUNG

Einstein once said that the most incomprehensible fact about nature was that it was comprehensible. It seems to me that the mysterious thing about nature is not that it is comprehensible but that it contains such a thing as comprehension at all.

JONATHAN MILLER

There is mystery and there is ignorance. We write from ignorance to discovery, but we do not "solve." The mystery remains.

MARVIN BELL

There is nothing more mysterious than a TV set left on in an empty room. It is even stranger than a man talking to himself or a woman standing dreaming at her stove.

JEAN BAUDRILLARD

NAMING

To name an object is largely to destroy poetic enjoyment.

MALLARME

Perhaps it would be best not to name it at all. Names are prone to vulgarization, to obsolescence.

HAROLD CLURMAN

To see is to forget the name of the thing one sees.

PAUL VALERY

Another way of approaching the thing is to consider it unnamed, unnamable.

PONGE

Primitive man regards his name as a vital portion of himself and guards it accordingly. Blackfoot Indians believe that they would be unfortunate in all their undertakings if they were to speak their names.

SIR JAMES FRAZER

Inside nothing they found a slip of the tongue. Inside the tongue a loose hair. Inside the hair, they found whatever is destroyed each time it is named.

CHARLES SIMIC

Yes, how curiously things do happen in life; were there not a bit of arrogance somewhere in it, one would indeed like very much to stand outside, confronting everything, that is, everything that occurs, so as surely not to lose anything. One would still remain fixed, perhaps for the first time really so, in the actual center of life, where everything comes together and has no name; – but then again, the names have bewitched us – the titles, the pretense of life – because the whole is too infinite, and we recover by calling it for a while by the name of one love, much as it is just this impassioned restriction that puts us in the wrong, makes us guilty, kills us....

RAINER MARIA RILKE

In Buddhist thought, there's the thing and there's the name for the thing and that's one thing too many.

LAURIE ANDERSON

It is disastrous to name ourselves.

WILLEM DE KOONING

The Japanese painter Hokusai changed his name sixty times, to celebrate each of his sixty births.

NO PROBLEM

There is no solution because there is no problem.

MARCEL DUCHAMP

Once, in the Orient, I talked of suicide with a sage whose clear and gentle eyes seemed forever to be gazing at a never-ending sunset. "Dying is no solution," he affirmed. "And living?" I asked. "Nor living either," he conceded. "But, who tells you there is a solution?"

ELIE WIESEL

For me, there is something other than, yes, no, and indifferent. It is for example the absence of investigations of this kind.

MARCEL DUCHAMP

If we live, we live; if we die, we die; if we suffer, we suffer; if we are terrified, we are terrified. There is no problem about it.

ALAN WATTS

The solution of the problem of life is seen in the vanishing of the problem. Is not this the reason why those who have found, after a long period of doubt, that the sense of life became clear, have then been unable to say what constituted that sense?

LUDWIG WITTGENSTEIN

The chief cause of problems is solutions.

ERIC SEVAREID

We feel that even if all possible scientific questions be answered, the problems of life have still not been touched at all. Of course there is then no question left, and just this is the answer. The solution of the problem of life is seen in the vanishing of this problem.

LUDWIG WITTGENSTEIN

NOTHING

Nothing is more real than nothing.

DEMOCRITUS

Every now and then it is possible to have absolutely nothing: the possibility of nothing.

JOHN CAGE

Every something is an echo of nothing.

Anything does go — but only when nothing is taken as the basis.

JOHN CAGE

When I have nothing left I will ask for no more.

ANTONIO PORCHIA

I was right not to be afraid of any thief but myself, who will end by leaving me nothing.

KATHERINE ANNE PORTER

I begin with what was always gone.

W.S. MERWIN

If it's not one thing, it's not another.

GARY DRAGER

…one bright moonlit night a messenger thrust a note into the anteroom where I was staying. On a sheet of magnificent scarlet paper I read the words, "there is nothing." It was the moonlight that made this so delightful; I wonder whether I would have enjoyed it at all on a rainy night.

THE PILLOW BOOK OF SEI SHONAGEN

"What are you thinking about, Bel-Gazou?" "Nothing, Mother."
An excellent answer. The same that I invariably gave when I was
her age.

COLETTE

God made everything out of nothing, but the nothingness
shows through.

PAUL VALERY

"Is there any point to which you would draw my attention?" "To
the curious incident of the dog in the nighttime." "The dog did
nothing in the nighttime." "That was the curious incident,"
remarked Sherlock Holmes.

ARTHUR CONAN DOYLE

If you haven't any lines in this scene with Kite you must find reasons for saying nothing.

WILLIAM GASKILL, WITH STAGE INSTRUCTIONS

It takes a long time to understand nothing.

EDWARD DAHLBERG

I thrive on nothingness.

ANDREW WYETH

"I see nobody on the road," said Alice. "I only wish I had such
eyes," the king remarked in a fretful tone. "To be able to see
nobody! And at that distance too! Why, it's as much as I can do
to see real people in this light."

LEWIS CARROLL

What we have caught and what we have killed we have left
behind, but what has escaped us we bring with us.

HERACLITUS

It was never there and already it's vanishing.

W.S. MERWIN

BREATHING ON YOUR OWN

Commitment, I feel prevents a man from developing. I am committed to non-commitment. In fact, I am wholly committed to everything I do.

FEDERICO FELLINI

Knowing that conscious decisions and personal memory are much too small a place to live, every human being streams at night into the loving nowhere.

RUMI

I have discovered that it is necessary, absolutely necessary, to believe in nothing. That is, we have to believe in something which has no form and no color – something which exists before all forms and colors appear.

SHUNRYU SUZUKI

I will take with me the emptiness of my hands. What you do not have you find everywhere.

W.S. MERWIN

It is never too late to do nothing.

ALLEN GINSBERG

There is not enough of nothing in it.

JOHN CAGE

Behind nothing, before nothing. This is the country of vertical time. I will leave you to add the zeroes.

LOREN EISELEY

Stop looking for what seems to be missing. You have everything you need to start with – nothing.

OBJECTS

The eagerness of objects to be what we are afraid to do cannot help but move us.

FRANK O'HARA

In the heaven of Indra, there is said to be a network of pearls, arranged that if you look at one you will see all the others reflected in it. In the same way each object in the world is not merely itself but involves every other object and in fact is everything else.

C. ELIOT

We all know the man whom children or dogs love instinctively. It is a rare gift to be able to inspire this affection. The fates have been kind to him. But to inspire the affection of inanimate things is something greater. The man to whom a collar or a window sash takes instinctively is a man who may truly be said to have luck on his side.

A. A. MILNE

There was a child went forth every day. And the first object he looked upon, that object he became.

WALT WHITMAN

ODDS AND ENDS

When the Duke of Wellington was asked by an admirer, "How did you really manage to beat Napoleon?" He replied simply, "Well, I'll tell you. Bonaparte's plans were made in wire, mine were made in string."

It's against the law in Oxford, Ohio, for a woman to undress in front of a photograph of a man.

NEWSPAPER

Team Finds Objects Older Than Light.

NEW YORK TIMES

A toad with four legs in front and six behind would be placed in a box with mirrors lining the four walls. The toad, amazed at its own appearance from every angle, would break into an oily sweat. This sweat would be collected and simmered for 3,972 days while being stirred with a willow branch. The result was the marvelous potion.

AKIRA KUROSAWA

Steps being taken to keep fireflies from going out.

NEWSPAPER HEADLINE

The same period that saw the rise of the public zoo saw the manufacture of the first stuffed animals.

MORRIS BERMAN

The British during World War II came up with some imaginative ideas. One was to freeze the clouds, move them along the coast of Southern England, and use them as platforms for anti-aircraft guns.

It's illegal in Salem, Va., to leave the house without knowing where you intend to go.

NEWSPAPER

It is interesting – that around 40000 BC man discovered at the same time how to draw, how to make fire and how to bury his dead.

ANDRÉ MALRAUX

Thousands of Red Army troops appeared never to have been in a big city before. They unscrewed light bulbs, and carefully packed them to take home, under the impression that they contained light and could be made to work anywhere.

CORNELIUS RYAN

Astronomer fears hostile attack: Would keep life on earth a secret.

Stay. There is something in the character of this place that makes an extra movie theatre unnecessary.

REAL ESTATE AD

Over his desk Robert Benchley had a five-foot shelf of books that were collected for their titles alone. Over the years, he acquired such items as: Forty Thousand Sublime and Beautiful Thoughts, Success With Small Fruits, Talks On Manure, Keeping A Single Cow, Bicycling For Ladies, The Culture and Disease of The Sweet Potato, Ailments of The Leg, In And Out With Mary Ann, Perverse Pussys.

In another entry, Mr. John Rabe wrote that with water and power failing and the city ringed with fire, he noticed that his canary, Peter, sang in rhythm to the sound of gunfire.

INVADING JAPANESE ARMY INTO CHINA

Uri Geller and a physicist were walking to the parking lot one day, and a large rock fell at their feet out of a clear blue sky. (In the eighteenth century, the French Academy passed a special resolution saying it would reject all further reports of rocks falling out of the sky.)

The three sisters were drawing all kinds of things beginning with the letter "Y": but could they draw all kinds? The Dormouse says they draw "mouse-traps, and the moon, and memory, and muchness – you know you say things are 'much of a muchness', – did you ever see such a thing as a drawing of a muchness?"

LEWIS CARROLL

Among these unfinished tales is that of Mr. James Phillimore, who, stepping back into his house to get his umbrella, was never more seen in this world.

ARTHUR CONAN DOYLE

141

Shakespeare couldn't have written Shakespeare if he'd had a typewriter.

Marcel Duchamp talked about his idea of "infra-thin". It had to do, in a decidedly nonscientific way, with infinitesimal spaces and subtle relationships. The space between the front and the back of paper was an example of "infra-thin", he said, and so was the sound made by his corduroy trousers rubbing together when he walked.

Message to deep-sea diver: "Surface at once. Ship is sinking."

Japanese psychologists claim they have taught pigeons how to tell a Picasso from a Monet with 90 per cent accuracy. However, the birds were not able to tell a Cezanne from a Renoir.

IVAN WEISS AND LYNN MUCKEN

Jean Gabin used to have a clause in his contract stipulating that he'd never have to open a door or bend over in any of his pictures.

My happiest experience in reading plays occurred during the Group Theatre days. A script had been submitted which began; "Act One: Ten thousand years before the creation of man. Act Two: Two weeks later."

HAROLD CLURMAN

OPINIONS

When Gandhi was asked what he thought of western civilization, he said, "It would be nice."

"Can't act. Can't sing. Balding. Can dance a little."

(MGM EXECUTIVE, REACTING TO FRED ASTAIRE'S SCREEN TEST. 1928.)

I detest my past and anyone else's. I detest resignation, patience, professional heroism and obligatory beautiful feelings. I also detest the decorative arts, folklore, advertising, voices making announcements, aerodynamism, boy scouts, the smell of mothballs, events of the moment, and drunken people.

RENÉ MAGRITTE

Nothing is more conducive to peace of mind than not having any opinion at all.

G.C. LICHTENBERG

Whatever it is, I'm against it.

GROUCHO MARX

Cabanne: One has the impression that every time you commit yourself to a position, you attenuate it by irony or sarcasm. Duchamp: I always do. Because I don't believe in positions. Cabanne: But what do you believe in? Duchamp: Nothing, of course. The word "belief" is another error. It's like the word "judgment." They're both horrible ideas, on which the world is based. I hope it won't be like that on the moon. I also don't believe in the word "being". The idea of being is a human invention.

ORDER/DISORDER

Writing a play is like smashing that ashtray, filming it in slow motion, and then running the film in reverse, so that the fragments of rubble appear to fly together. You start – or at least I start – with the rubble.

TOM STOPPARD

It is the material of all things loose and set afloat that makes my sea.

HERMAN MELVILLE

Order, unity and continuity are human inventions, just as truly as catalogues and encyclopedias.

BERTRAND RUSSELL

Anything which is entirely beyond my control fascinates me and seems to me to have some awful and particular significance, so that, while I was frightened, I was pleased also.

EVELYN SCOTT

It is a paradox of nature that such random processes can produce regular forms, and that regular processes often produce random forms.

LEOPOLD AND LANGBEIN

(Otto Neugebauer, the historian of ancient mathematics, told a story about the boy Einstein) As he was a late talker, his parents were worried. At last, at the supper table one night, he broke his silence to say, "The soup is too hot." Greatly relieved, his parents asked why he had never said a word before. Albert replied, "Because up to now everything was in order."

I have known tailors who sew beautiful clothes by tearing them to pieces.

RUMI

A. A violent order is disorder: and B. A great disorder is an order. These two things are one.

WALLACE STEVENS

Since we value – and madly overvalue – whatever is ordered, we tend to impute order to whatever we value.

If I were about to start to build a platform, I think I'd start with ash.

CYNTHIA MACDONALD

PARADOX/CONTRADICTIONS

Be obscure clearly.

E.B. WHITE

I fear in myself only those contradictions with a tendency toward reconciliation.

RAINER MARIA RILKE

James Thurber once sat by his window watching men cut down elm trees to clear a site for an institution in which to confine people who had been driven insane by the cutting down of elm trees.

Experience a minute. Experience an hour. Can you experience a minute and an hour together simultaneously, at the same time. This is an important question to ask.

JOHN BROCKMAN

When television came roaring in after the war (World War II) they did a little school survey asking children which they preferred and why – television or a radio. And there was this 7-year-old boy who said be preferred radio "because the pictures were better."

ALISTAIR COOKE

I force myself into self-contradiction to avoid following my taste.

MARCEL DUCHAMP

How have I managed to come back here so many times without ever going away?

ANTONIO PORCHIA

My mind never changes. but I change my mind whenever I wish.

GAYAN VODAN NIRTAN

Here are your tea things. No water in the tap. No tea. No sugar. No cup or saucer. No spoon. No glass. No bread and no jam.

PABLO PICASSO

You can only know after you've been it... and in order to be it you've got to give up knowing you know. It's a fantastic paradox.

RAM DASS

The formula "two and two make five" is not without its attraction.

FEODOR DOSTOYEVSKY

One should not think slightingly of the paradoxical, for the paradox is the source of the thinker's passion, and the thinker without a paradox is like a lover without a feeling, a paltry mediocrity. The supreme paradox of all thought is the attempt to discover something that thought cannot think.

SÖREN KIERKEGAARD

We labor under a number of delusions, one of which is that life makes sense; i.e., that we are sane. We persist in this view despite massive evidence to the contrary. We live fragmented, compartmentalized lives in which contradictions are carefully sealed off from each other. We have been taught to think linearly rather than comprehensively.

EDWARD HALL

Our interest's on the dangerous edge of things. The honest thief, the tender murderer, the superstitious atheist.

MARGARET LAURENCE

Perhaps the most significant clarification is the simultaneity of the oppositions in the creative mind. When creators conceive of simultaneous opposites, they're not flipping from one opposition to another or even resolving the opposites into synthesis or reconciliation of opposites. The thinking is quite different because it may consist of a paradox which is intrinsically unresolvable, unreconcilable, and unsusceptible to synthesis.

ALBERT ROTHENBURG

Everything resolves itself in contradiction.

SÖREN KIERKEGAARD

Just because everything is different doesn't mean anything has changed.

IRENE POTTER

Everytime I hear a fire engine it seems like the trucks are running away from the fire. Not towards it.

LAURIE ANDERSON

It gets late early here.

YOGI BERRA

I can't hear myself hearing.

MARCEL DUCHAMP

If I want to turn right, I first turn left, then sadly edge rightwards.

FRANZ KAFKA

PASSION

When you're learning, you're burning – putting out a lot of heat. When you're all burned up, then you become light.

DA FREE JOHN

For years I was tuned a few notes too high – I don't see how I could stand it!

WILLIAM STAFFORD

No trace: When you do something, you should burn yourself completely, like a good bonfire, leaving no trace of yourself.

SUZUKI

The price of passion is no passion.

JOHN FOWLES

On some hill of despair the bonfire you kindle can light the great sky – though it's true of course to make it burn you have to throw yourself in....

GALWAY KINNELL

But you know, what really moved me most, I think, was Dante's passage through Purgatorio on the way to Paradisio. The people there in Purgatorio were inside their flames expurgating their errors and sins. And there was one particular incident… that was when Dante was talking to a spirit, an unknown woman in her flame. And as she answered Dante's questions, like all the other spirits, she had to step out of her flame to talk to him, until at last this unknown feminine spirit was compelled to say to Dante: "Would you please hurry up with your questions so I can get on with my burning?"

T.S. ELIOT

If I could only remember that the days were not bricks to be laid row on row, to be built into a solid house, where one might dwell in safety and peace, but only food for the fires of the heart, the fires which keep the poet alive as the citizen never lives, which burn all the roofs of security.

EDMUND WILSON

How many things here (because I imagine that I know them) fail to move me as much.

RAINER MARIA RILKE

I want something cool to press on all the places I'm burning. Ice roses beneath my hair.

LYN LIFSHIN

What is to give light must endure burning.

VICTOR FRANKEL

I learned to trust my obsessions. It is surely a great calamity for a human being to have no obsessions.

ROBERT BLY

Every morning I jump out of bed and step on a landmine. The landmine is me. After the explosion, I spend the rest of the day putting the pieces together.

RAY BRADBURY

You've heard the saying: "Kiss the flame and it is yours?"

THOMAS LUX

Like a harp burning on an island nobody knows about.

JAMES TATE

My body was a lovely bonfire burning night and day on that tropical coast.

PABLO NERUDA

Passion doesn't fade. It must be suppressed.

RUMI

PAST/FUTURE

The future is now – it's just not evenly distributed.

WILLIAM GIBSON

The future is but the obsolete in reverse.

VLADIMIR NABOKOV

Isn't it amazing the way the future succeeds in creating an appropriate past?

JOHN LEONARD

For example, everyone automatically assumes that the present is the result of the past. Turn it around, and consider whether the past may not be a result of the present. The past may be streaming back from the now, like the country as seen from an airplane.

ALAN WATTS

Tying his tie and whistling a tune Zimmer strikes a nostalgic note and invents his past.

ANNIE DILLARD

BREATHING ON YOUR OWN

Being on time when the rest of the world is behind gives the impression of being ahead.

JEAN-LUC GODARD

Let's reminisce about tomorrow.

EDWIN NEWMAN

Maps flapping on the walls, the walls falling in and me waiting as usual while the future limps from door to door.

RICHARD SHELTON

The years come to my door and knock and walk away sighing.

TILLINGHAST

The future is something which everyone reaches at the rate of sixty minutes an hour.

C.S. LEWIS

This is the end of the past. Be happy.

(He is a slave to the past) He is like the soldier who shouted to his captain that he had taken a prisoner. "Bring him here, then," said the captain. "I can't," said the man. "He won't let go of me."

Nostalgia isn't what it used to be.

GRAFFITI

We must work at the future as weavers work at high-warp tapestry: without seeing it.

ANATOLE FRANCE

Invent a past for the present.

DANIEL STERN

Psychologically speaking there is no tomorrow: We have invented it.

KRISHNAMURTI

The one charm of the past is that it is past.

OSCAR WILDE

But tomorrow is over so what can I do with today coming as it does at the wrong time.

RICHARD SHELTON

We are the echo of the future.

W.S. MERWIN

One of the schools of Tilon has reached the point of denying time. It reasons that the present is undefined, that the future has no other reality than as present hope, that the past is no more than the present memory. Another school declares that the whole of time has already happened and that our life is a vague memory or dim reflection, doubtless false and fragmented, of an irrevocable process.

JORGE LUIS BORGES

PENCIL/ERASER

My pencils outlast their erasers.

VLADIMIR NABOKOV

As though naturally erasers would speak the language of pencils.

HOWARD NEMEROV

It is as if I were attempting to trace with the point of a pencil the shadow of the tracing pencil.

NATHANAEL WEST

It could be that there's only one word and it's all we need. It's here in this pencil. Every pencil in the world is like this.

W.S. MERWIN

The night nurse is passing out the evening pills. She walks on two erasers.

ANNE SEXTON

One day when I was studying with Schoenberg, he pointed out the eraser on his pencil and said, "This end is more important than the other."

JOHN CAGE

PERCEPTION

And he told about an interview he had once with Barney Oldfield, the great racing driver. He had asked Oldfield why he always seemed to be involved in automobile accidents when driving in street traffic. Oldfield replied that he was never able to think clearly when traveling at less than a hundred miles an hour.

Give up the word "is."

Whatever one believes to be true either is true or becomes true in one's own mind within limits to be determined experimentally and experientially. These limits themselves are, in turn, beliefs to be transcended.

JOHN LILLY

One thinks one is tracing the outline of the thing's nature over and over again, and one is merely tracing round the frame through which we look at it.

LUDWIG WITTGENSTEIN

Reminder: What am I doing on a level of consciousness where this is real?

I work from awkwardness. By that I mean I don't like to arrange things. If I stand in front of something, instead of arranging it, I arrange myself.

DIANE ARBUS

We say "seeing is believing," but actually, as Santayana pointed out, we are all much better at believing than at seeing. In fact, we are seeing what we believe nearly all the time and only occasionally seeing what we can't believe.

ROBERT ANTON WILSON

The real reality is there, but everything you know about "it" is in your mind and yours to do with as you like. Conceptualization is art, and you are the artist.

ROBERT ANTON WILSON

As a special treat, a teacher took her class to visit the Museum of Natural History. The children returned home very excited, and rushing into his house, one of the little boys greeted his mother exuberantly, saying, "What do you think we did today, Mother! The teacher took us to a dead circus."

I wouldn't have believed it if I hadn't seen it, (but more neuro-physiologically precise to say) I wouldn't have seen it at all, if I hadn't already believed it in the first place.

LYALL WATSON

I am reminded of the anecdote of the little old lady who when offered an opportunity to look at the moon through a telescope, commented, when she had done so, "Give me the moon as God made it."

JOSEPH CAMPBELL

Everyone who believes what he sees is a mystic.

The Working Brain: We often think that when we have completed our study of one we know all about two, because "two" is "one and one." We forget that we still have to make a study of "and."

A. EDDINGTON

Mr. S.B., blind from the age of ten months, his sight returned when he was over fifty: S. B. was astonished to see a crescent moon, and asked what it was. He had always imagined the quarter moon would look like a quarter piece of cake.

If a pickpocket meets a holy man, he will see only his pockets.

HARI DASS BABA

Once, when a GI was visiting Picasso during the liberation of France, he said that he could not understand the artists' paintings. "Why do you paint a person looking from the side and from the front at the same time?" Picasso asked, "Do you have a girl-friend?" "Yes," replied the soldier. "Do you have a picture of her?" The soldier pulled from his wallet a photograph of the girl. Picasso looked at it in mock astonishment and asked, "Is she so small?"

I'm afraid that if you look at it thing long enough, it loses all of it's meaning.

ANDY WARHOL

People who look through keyholes are apt to get the idea that most things are keyhole shaped.

If angels did not exist I would have to invent them. Which comes, perhaps, to the same thing.

ANTHONY TOWNE

Once we know one, we believe we know two, because one plus one equals two – We forget that beforehand, we must know the meaning of plus.

JEAN-LUC GODARD

BREATHING ON YOUR OWN

And see, no longer blinded by our eyes.

RUPERT BROOKE

As for the other… beware, as they say, of mistaking the finger for the moon when you're pointing at it.

JOHN CAGE

A person can look at pointing in reverse, that is, from finger tip to wrist.

LUDWIG WITTGENSTEIN

Be careful how you interpret life, it is that way.

ERICH HELLER

Perhaps to our senses things offer only their rejections. Perfume is what the flowers throw away.

PAUL VALERY

To see an aquarium, better not be a fish.

ANDRÉ MALRAUX

If the doors of perception were cleansed everything would appear to man as it is, infinite.

WILLIAM BLAKE

He who goes up step by step always finds himself level with a step.

ANTONIO PORCHIA

One and one make two. That's great. What's a two?

BILL COSBY

If the only tool you have is a hammer, you tend to see every problem as a nail.

ABRAHAM MASLOW

The question is not what you look at but what you see.

HENRY DAVID THOREAU

New organs of perception come into being because of necessity. So, necessitous one, increase your need.

RUMI

A glazier repaired fifty windows before he realized he had a crack in his glasses.

We dull our lives by the way we conceive them.

JAMES HILLMAN

Lost between decks on the great Atlantic liner only an hour after putting to sea, McCormick had to look for help to find his cabin. "What was the number?" asked the steward. "I couldn't tell you," said McCormick, "but I'd know it because it had a lighthouse outside the porthole."

Exterior perception is truthful hallucination.

HIPPOLYTE TAIME

Those who wear clothes look to the launderer.

RUMI

The artist Robert Morris once created a piece in which he employed the services of a woman blind from birth to draw while he spoke instructions to her. At one point in the execution of the piece, he tried to explain perspective to her. "Objects further away appear smaller than closer ones," he said. "That," she replied, "is the most ridiculous thing I've ever heard."

PHIL PATTON

Your consciousness is your contribution to reality. What you perceive as real becomes real.

RUMI

There ain't nothing that happens to a person that isn't that person. The world out there only does what you tell it to do, The world is happening to you the way it is happening because you're telling yourself the story that way.

TOM SPANBAUER

Ed Wynn about girls on television. "What's funny about a three-inch girl?"

The final belief is to believe in a fiction, which you know to be a fiction, there being nothing else. The exquisite truth is to know that it is a fiction and that you believe it willingly.

WALLACE STEVENS

He lies like an eyewitness.

RUSSIAN SAYING

One fingertip hides the moon – the whole world may be hidden from view by a single point.

RUMI

What does the swallow know of the owl's insomnia?

MARK STRAND

We have to remember that what we observe is not nature itself, but rather nature exposed to our methods of questioning.

LUDWIG WITTGENSTEIN

Every second is a door to eternity. The door is opened by perception.

RUMI

To know the world one must construct it.

CESARE PAVESE

Much study in the present period has been devoted to the way our language affects, and in part determines, what we can perceive and how we organize our perceptions. It is interesting to speculate how different the world must have looked before Thomas Gray coined the word "picturesque" in 1740 or before Whewell coined "scientist" in the 19th century (or before Shakespeare coined the words "assassination" "disgraceful" or "lonely.")

I once asked a young boy how it happened that one sock he was wearing was white and the other one brown. "Oh, that's the way they are," he reassured me; "I have another pair at home just like it."

BEREL LANG

PERFECTION

Perfection is laziness.

JOHN CAGE

Whatever I take, I take too much or too little; I do not take the exact amount. The exact amount is no use to me.

ANTONIO PORCHIA

Nothing is more imprecise than precision.

EUGENE IONESCO

Perfectionism is spelled PARALYSIS.

WINSTON CHURCHILL

I play just well enough for perfection, while virtuosos play too well for perfection.

NED ROREM

A teacher asks the boy what two plus two equals. "Four" the child responds. "Very good, Robert." "Very good, the child says indignantly. Very good! It's perfect."

NEWSPAPER

PERMANENCE

In the word "Buddha," even the letter B is nothing but dust.

KYODO ROSHI

All composite things decay: work out your salvation with diligence.

THE BUDDHA

Only the ephemeral is of lasting value.

EUGENE IONESCO

Anything you can think of is likely to pass away.

RUMI

PHILOSOPHY

That's why I love philosophy: no one wins.

SHUNRYU SUZUKI

The Chinese say that when you have too much trouble, you write poetry. There are two kinds of poetry; in one you jump in, in the other you jump out. If you jump out you become a philosopher. If you jump in you die with the poem.

A newspaperman wrote asking me to send him my philosophy in a nutshell. "Get out of whatever cage you happen to be in."

JOHN CAGE

One day, someone showed me a glass of water that was half full. And he said, "Is it half full or half empty," So I drank the water. No more problem.

ALEJANDRO JODOROWSKY

The results of philosophy are the uncovering of one or another piece of plain nonsense and of bumps that the understanding has got by running its head up against the limits of language.

LUDWIG WITTGENSTEIN

I have a simple philosophy: Fill what's empty. Empty what's full. Scratch where it itches.

ALICE ROOSEVELT LONGWORTH

The philosopher Gabriel Marcel was lecturing to a group of American Logical Positivists on grace and transcendence. They kept telling him to speak more clearly and to "say what he meant." Finally Marcel paused and then said, "I guess I can't explain it to you. But if I had a piano here, I could play it."

Some days, you win. Some days, you lose. And some days, it rains.

BASEBALL PROVERB

PHOTOGRAPHY

I don't take the photograph. The photograph takes me.

HENRI CARTIER-BRESSON

Actually, I'm not all that interested in the subject of photography. Once the picture is in the box, I'm not all that interested in what happens next. Hunters, after all, usually aren't cooks.

HENRI CARTIER-BRESSON

We must be lost soon in the elementary Kodak experiment.

LEONARD COHEN

Balzac's dread of being photographed was that... everybody in their natural state was made up of a series of ghostly images superimposed in layers to infinity, wrapped in infinitesimal films... each Daguerrian operation was therefore going to lay hold of, detach, and use up one of the layers of the body on which it focused.

And what advice would you give an aspiring photographer? "To fall in love." Lartigue replied.

JACQUES HENRI

A hundredth of a second here, a hundredth of a second there — even if you put them end to end they still only add up to one, two, perhaps three seconds snatched from eternity.

ROBERT DOISNEAU

POETRY

I know poetry is indispensable, but to what?

JEAN COCTEAU

Publishing a volume of poetry is like dropping a rose-petal down the Grand Canyon and waiting for the echo.

DON MARQUIS

Poetry is that stuff in books which doesn't quite reach to the margin.

SCHOOLCHILD

I am not interested in grasping precisely a man I know. I am interested only in exaggerating him precisely.

ELIAS CANETTI

A poem is a serious joke, a truth that has learned jujitsu.

WILLIAM STAFFORD

If Galileo had said in verse that the world moved, the inquisition might have let him alone.

THOMAS HARDY

Mallarme thought it was the job of poetry, using words, to clean up our word-clogged reality – by creating silences around things.

Poetry is a raid on the inarticulate.

T.S. ELIOT

My method is simple: not to mix myself into poetry. It must come of itself. Even to hear its name whispered frightens it away. I try to make a table. It's up to you thereafter to eat off it, question it, or make firewood out of it.

JEAN COCTEAU

Wanted: a needle swift enough to sew this poem into a blanket.

CHARLES SIMIC

The poem that has stolen these words from my mouth may not be this poem.

MARK STRAND

A poem is always married to someone.

RENÉ CHAR

Poetry is just the evidence of life. If your life is burning well, poetry is just the ash.

LEONARD COHEN

The poet turns defeat into victory, victory into defeat, indifferently.

RENÉ CHAR

The poem. It is a piece of meat carried by a burglar to distract a watchdog.

CHARLES SIMIC

And what, after all, is the poem but the constant threading of a needle? You have used the same thread over and over, sewing clouds, sewing a damaged heart, perfecting the things you know well.

NORMAN ROSTEN

Poetry is not an occupation, but a verdict.

LEONARD COHEN

In vain have oceans been squandered on you – and still, and still, you have not written the poem.

Poetry, like the moon, does not advertise anything.

WILLIAM BLISSETT

The poet doesn't invent. He listens.

JEAN COCTEAU

The poem is the point at which our strength gave out.

RICHARD ROSEN

I always used to think it was the poet's gift to make other people's possessions clearer and more visible to them, merely by his presence.

RAINER MARIA RILKE

And me, I am writing a poem for you. Look! No hands.

RUTH KRAUSS

The Chinese say that poetry is the direction of your will. If that is not enough, you add a sigh. If that does not express what you mean completely, you chant or sing it. If that is not enough, you move your arms and legs too; you dance. That is poetry.

Poetry is what gets lost in translation.

ROBERT FROST

A true poet does not bother to be poetical. Nor does a nursery gardener scent his roses.

JEAN COCTEAU

It is extremely important that great poetry be written but it is a matter of indifference who writes it.

EZRA POUND

The great mathematician David Hilbert praised a new student of his who seemed to show great promise. Some time later Ernst Cassirer asked him what had happened to this student. Hilbert replied, "Oh, he did not have enough imagination to be a mathematician, so he became a poet!"

On one day in the week, if possible, neither read nor write poetry.

CHINESE RULE OF HEALTH.

The trouble with most poetry is that it is either subjective or objective.

BASHO

That is how one should read all books of poetry. Along the border, a short way into the woods and then back into the summer sun.

RAINER MARIA RILKE

A good poet is someone who manages, in a lifetime of standing out in thunderstorms, to be struck by lightning five or six times.

RANDALL JARRELL

Your eyelash will write on my cheek the poem that hasn't been thought of.

RUMI

Writing poems is easy, like swimming into a fish net.

WILLIAM STAFFORD

Poetry is the kind of thing you have to see from the corner of your eye. If you look straight at it you can't see it, but if you look a little to one side it is there.

WILLIAM STAFFORD

Poets don't draw. They unravel their handwriting and then tie it up again, but differently.

JEAN COCTEAU

There is poetry in everything. That is the biggest argument against poetry.

A. ALVAREZ

POSSESSIONS

Not being able to say, "This is mine," we'll want when we inquire to get no response at all.

JOHN CAGE

Things that I longed for in vain and things that I got – let them pass. Let me but truly possess the things that I ever spurned and overlooked.

Complete possession is proved by giving. All you are unable to give possesses you.

ANDRÉ GIDE

There is poetry as soon as we realize that we possess nothing.

JOHN CAGE

I went to the Doctor. "I feel lost, blind with love. What should I do?" Give up owning things and being somebody. Quit existing.

RUMI

PRESENT

Real generosity toward the future consists in giving all to what is present.

ALBERT CAMUS

Death is always in the here and now; it can never happen in the future. Can you die in the future? You can die only in the present. No one has ever died in the future.

RAJNEESH

There is nothing more surprising than right now. Right now is where you always are anyway.

JAMES BROUGHTON

You phone the Time Lady and listen to her tell the minutes and seconds, then adjust all the clocks in the house so their hands reach midnight together. You must like listening to the Time Lady because she is a recording you don't have to talk to. Also she distinctly names the present moment, never slipping into the past or sliding into the future.

MAXINE HONG KINGSTON

The present is the only thing that has no end.

ERWIN SCHRODINGER

The absolute tranquility is the present moment. Though it is at this moment, there is no limit to this moment, and therein is eternal delight.

HUI-NENG

Today is obsolete.

WALTER LOWENFELS

The today that never comes on time.

OCTAVIO PAZ

PROGRESS

The feeling we are getting nowhere – that is a pleasure that will continue.

JOHN CAGE

All progress is based upon a universal innate desire on the part of any organism to live beyond its income.

SAMUEL BUTLER

Progress in itself is not always positive, disease progresses.

NED ROREM

The fifteen-year-old daughter of a friend once addressed the old Jung as follows: "Herr Professor, you are so clever. Could you please tell me the shortest path to my life's goal?" Without a moments hesitation Jung replied, "The detour!"

Anything which is really new to us is by that fact automatically traditional.

T.S. ELIOT

QUESTIONS/ANSWERS

Jean-Pierre Aumont says to Andre Gide, "May I ask you an indiscreet question?" To which Gide replies, "There are no indiscreet questions, there are only indiscreet answers."

My whole life is waiting for the questions to which I have prepared answers.

TOM STOPPARD

If I could learn the word for yes it could teach me questions.

W.S. MERWIN

Questions are fiction, and answers are anything from more fiction to science-fiction.

SAUL STEINBERG

May I ask you a highly personal question? It's what life does all the time.

KURT VONNEGUT JR.

Answers are just echoes, they say. But a question travels before it comes back, and that counts.

WILLIAM STAFFORD

There are works which wait, and which one does not understand for a long time; the reason is that they bring answers to questions which have not yet been raised; for the question often arrives a terribly long time after the answer.

OSCAR WILDE

Be patient toward all that is unsolved in your heart and try to love the questions themselves. Do not seek the answers, which cannot be given you because you would not be able to live them. And the point is, to live everything. Live the questions now. Perhaps you will then gradually, without noticing it, live along some distant day into the answer.

RAINER MARIA RILKE

"What is the answer?" asked Gertrude Stein on her deathbed. There was silence, "Well, then what is the question?" – and she died.

There's a wonderful story in a paper by Daisetz Suzuki. The young student said to his master, "Am I in possession of Buddha consciousness?" The master said, "No." The student said, "Well, I've been told that all things are in the possession of Buddha consciousness, the rocks, the tree, the butterflies, the birds, the animals, all beings." The master said, "You are correct. All things are in possession of Buddha consciousness. The rocks, the trees, the butterflies, the bees, the birds, the animals, all beings – but not you." "Not me? Why not?" "Because you are asking this question."

When the answer cannot be put into words, neither can the question be put into words.

LUDWIG WITTGENSTEIN

But they are useless. They can only give you answers.

(PICASSO ABOUT COMPUTERS)

"To be or not to be" is not the question; it's the answer.

FRED ALAN WOLF

When composing one of his symphonies, Gustav Mahler felt not so much that all his deepest questions had been answered as that there were no longer any questions to be asked.

It's a question too complicated to answer if you put me up against a wall. And too simple to ask.

PENELOPE GILLIATT

If love is the answer, could you rephrase the question?

LILY TOMLIN

Interviewer: "I've got lots of questions to ask you." Yogi Berra: "If you ask me anything I don't know, I'm not going to answer."

QUIET/STILL

You do not need to leave your room. Remain sitting at your table and listen. Do not even listen, simply wait. Do not even wait, be quite still and solitary. The world will freely offer itself to you to be unmasked, it has no choice, it will roll in ecstasy at your feet.

FRANZ KAFKA

The base of the lighthouse is dark.

OLD JAPANESE PROVERB.

You must learn to be still in the midst of activity and to be vibrantly alive in repose.

INDIRA GANDHI

The sole cause of man's unhappiness is that he does not know how to stay quietly in his room.

BLAISE PASCAL

Patience is also a form of action.

AUGUSTE RODIN

Now it is time for you not to do what you always do. Sit here until we leave and not-do.

CARLOS CASTANEDA

A little while alone in your room will prove more valuable than anything else that could ever be given you.

RUMI

I have so often asked myself whether the days on which we are compelled to be idle aren't the very ones we spend in the deepest activity? Whether our actions themselves, when they come later, are not merely the last afterring of a great movement that takes place in us on inactive days?

RAINER MARIA RILKE

"Don't just do something," Buddha said, "stand there!"

DANIEL BERRIGAN

Not activity. Not reasoning. Not calculating. Not busy behavior of any kind. Not reading. Not talking. Not making an effort. Not thinking. Simply bearing in mind what it is one needs to know.

G. SPENCER BROWN

Each song is love's stillness. Each star is time's stillness, a knot of time. Each sigh is the stillness of the shriek.

FEDERICO GARCIA LORCA

Joseph Conrad lamented: "I begrudge each minute I spend away from paper. Inspiration comes to me while looking at the paper. Not writing, but just looking at the paper."

How can we become still? By moving with the stream.

TAO TE CHING

REALITY/ILLUSION

When his psychiatrist urged him to struggle with reality, he responded: "Doctor, I wrestled with reality for 40 years and I am happy to state that I finally won out over it!"

EDWARD F. DOWD

Reality is only a Rorschach inkblot, you know.

ALAN WATTS

What is most admirable in the fantastic is that the fantastic doesn't exist; all is real.

ANDRE BRETON

Disillusion is the last illusion.

WALLACE STEVENS

Then you could be eligible for such an ineffable compliment as the one that a lady paid to the sculpture of David Tolerton: "Is it real," she asked, "or did you make it?"

JOHN CAGE

Go, go, go said the bird: human kind cannot bear very much reality.

T.S. ELIOT

Everything that does not need you is real.

W.S. MERWIN

A certain selection and discretion must be used in producing a realistic effect.

ARTHUR CONAN DOYLE

One of the definitions of sanity is the ability to tell real from unreal. Soon we'll need a new definition.

ALVIN TOFFLER

Maybe reality isn't all I imagine it to be.

The more poetic, the more real. This is the core of my philosophy.

NOVALIS

I see no dividing line between imagination and reality.

FEDERICO FELLINI

It is respectable to have no illusions – and safe – and profitable and dull.

JOSEPH CONRAD

I refuse to be intimidated by reality. What is reality anyway? Reality is nothing but a collective hunch.

LILY TOMLIN

Reality is not always probable, or likely.

JORGE LUIS BORGES

She said the hardest thing to teach her three-year-old child was what was alive and what wasn't. The phone rings and she holds it out to her kid and says, "It's Grandma. Talk to Grandma." But she's holding a piece of plastic. And the kid says to herself: "Wait a minute. Is the phone alive? Is the TV alive? What about that radio? What is alive in this room and what doesn't have life?"

LAURIE ANDERSON

Worshipping the teapot instead of drinking the tea.

WEI WU WEI

"What-is-this?" the Unicorn asked. "This is a child!" Haigha replied eagerly, coming in front of Alice to introduce her. "I always thought they were fabulous monsters!" said the Unicorn. "Is it alive?" "It can talk," said Haigha solemnly. The Unicorn looked dreamily at Alice, and said: "Talk, child." Alice said: "Do you know, I always thought Unicorns were fabulous monsters too. I never saw one alive before." "Well, now that we have seen each other," said the Unicorn, "if you'll believe in me, I'll believe in you. Is that a bargain?"

LEWIS CARROLL

Realism is a corruption of reality.

WALLACE STEVENS

We quietly wait. The wind keeps telling us something we want to pass on to the world: Even far things are real.

WILLIAM STAFFORD

Put these pages in the fire, I beg you; in being kept, they become less real.

PABLO NERUDA

Cloquet hated reality but realized it was still the only place to get a good steak.

WOODY ALLEN

I do take one hundred per cent seriously that the world is a figment of the imagination.

JOHN WHEELER, PHYSICIST

I know that nothing has ever been real without my beholding it. All becoming has needed me. My looking ripens things and they come toward me, to meet and be met.

RAINER MARIA RILKE

After an hour or so in the woods looking for mushrooms, Dad said, "Well, we can always go and buy some real ones."

JOHN CAGE

Reality is not what it is. It consists of the many realities which it can be made into.

WALLACE STEVENS

From my disinherited mother I learned to stay alive by dreaming myself into existence. From her I learned that everything is real. It was a lesson of enormous value to me.

JAMAKE HIGHWATER

RESPONSIBILITY

If you are to be, you must begin by assuming responsibility. You alone are responsible for every moment of your life, for every one of your acts.

ANTOINE DE SAINT-EXUPERY

It's true that I've driven through a number of red lights. But on the other hand, I've stopped at a lot of green ones I've never gotten credit for.

GLENN GOULD

It matters immensely. The slightest sound matters. The most momentary rhythm matters. You can do as you please, yet everything matters.

WALLACE STEVENS

I think we are responsible for the universe, but that doesn't mean we decide anything.

RENÉ MAGRITTE

Responsibility is to keep the ability to respond.

GUSTAV MAHLER

SAVE FROM A FIRE

Question: If your house were on fire, which object would you take with you? Tristan Bernard: The thing nearest the door.

If there were a fire in your studio what would you save? Alberto Giacometti: My cat, and then I would let it go.

If you had to save your works from a fire, which would you save? Pablo Neruda: Possibly none of them. What am I going to need them for? I would rather like to save a girl… or a good collection of detective stories… which would entertain me much more than my own poetry.

If you had to save your works from a fire, which would you save? Jean Cocteau: The fire, of course.

SCIENCE

The energy you use to turn a single page of a book is more than all the radio telescopes have collected since the beginning of radio astronomy.

JOCELYN BELL BURNELL

It's a good thing that geometry was invented before the creation of the world, because then the world could not have been made.

EUGENE VIOLLET-LE-DUC

Animals studied by Americans rush about frantically, with an incredible display of hustle and pep, and at last achieve the desired result by chance. Animals observed by Germans sit still and think, and at last evolve the solution out of their inner consciousness.

BERTRAND RUSSELL

The capacity to blunder slightly is the real marvel of DNA. Without this special attribute, we would still be anaerobic bacteria and there would be no muse.

LEWIS THOMAS

Space isn't remote at all. It's only an hour's drive away if your car could go straight upwards.

SIR FRED HOYLE

You know that, according to quantum theory, if two particles collide with enough energy you can, in principle, with an infinitesimal probability, produce two grand pianos.

I.I. RABI

I knew of a physicist at the University of Chicago who was rather crazy like some scientists, and the idea of the insolidity, the instability of the physical world impressed him so much that he used to go around in enormous padded slippers for fear he should fall through the floor.

ALAN WATTS

The story is told of a scientist who removed one leg of his test animal each time the animal hurdled over a barrier. After removing all four legs, the scientist concluded that the animal's failure to perform was evidence of a memory deficit.

If you take a single atom and make it as large as Yankee Stadium, it would consist almost entirely of empty space. The center of the atom, the nucleus, would be smaller than a baseball sitting out in center field. The outer parts of the atom would be tiny gnats buzzing about at an altitude higher than any pop fly Babe Ruth ever hit. And between the baseball and the gnats? Nothingness. All empty. You are more emptiness than anything else. Indeed, if all the space were taken out of you, you would be a million times smaller than the smallest grain of sand.

BRIAN SWIMME

In fact, I've come to the conclusion that I never did know anything about it.

THOMAS EDISON, ON ELECTRICITY

The ultimate fraud is the scientific atheist who believes in probability.

BART KOSKO

The information necessary reliably to assemble a human being fits on a DNA molecule weighing less than the ink in the period at the end of this sentence.

FRANK WILCZEK AND BETSY DEVINE

The physicist Wolfgang Pauli once remarked about a speculative proposal in physics: "It's not even wrong."

We take a blue billiard ball and shrink it to one-thousandth of its original size. It is now like a mote in a sunbeam to use Verdic language. We shrink it another million times. It is now completely out of the see-touch reality. Color is caused by the reflection of a particular wavelength of light in that range to which our eyes are sensitive. Our shrunken billiard ball is now smaller than these wavelengths. It cannot reflect light. What is its color? It has none, It does not even have an absence of color. The term simply does not apply.

LESHEN AND MORGENAN

SECRET

A photograph is a secret about a secret. The more it tells you the less you know.

DIANE ARBUS

Don't call yourself a secret unless you mean to keep it.

LEONARD COHEN

There are no secrets except the secrets that keep themselves.

SHAW

Each thing we see hides something else we want to see.

RENÉ MAGRITTE

SELF IMAGE

Many people's sense of worth, the value they place on the image of the self, is directly related to the number of situations in which they are in control, which means that many people have a problem with their self-image, because they are in control of so little.

EDWARD HALL

Trying to define yourself is like trying to bite your own teeth.

ALAN WATTS

Narcissism: When one grows too old to believe in one's uniqueness, one falls in love with one's complexity – as if layers of lies could replace the green illusion; or the sophistries of failure, the stench of success.

JOHN FOWLES

Angels fly because they take themselves lightly.

JEAN COCTEAU OF MISIA SERT

It is not only the most difficult thing to know oneself, but the most inconvenient one, too.

H. W. SHAW

I will not be other than I am: I find too much content in my condition: I am always caressed.

A YOUNG FRENCH WITCH, C. 1660

178

7

According to the Oxford English Dictionary, it was not until 1674 that the word "self" took on its modern meaning; self-sufficient 1598; self-knowledge 1613; self-made 1615; self-seeker 1632; selfish 1640; self-examination 1647; self-interest 1649; self-knowing 1667; self-deception 1677; self-determination 1683; self-conscious 1687.

SHADOWS

Nothing in the universe can travel at the speed of light, they say, forgetful of the shadow's speed.

HOWARD NEMEROV

I want what I love to continue to live, so that you can reach everything my love directs you to, so that my shadow can travel along in your hair, so that everything can learn the reason for my song.

PABLO NERUDA

To confront a person with his shadow is to show him his own light.

CARL JUNG

Between the idea and the reality... falls the shadow.

T.S. ELIOT

There is someone who looks after us from behind the curtain. In truth, we are not here. This is our shadow.

RUMI

She knew two herons flew over each morning, and sent their shadows along the ground below them. She would wake early and run after their shadows, trying to keep in their shade!

WISHING BONE CYCLE

Is the possibility of movement like a shadow of the movement itself?

LUDWIG WITTGENSTEIN

During the day the shadows sleep. At night they dance in the darkness.

FLORINDA DONNER

No matter how fast you run, your shadow more than keeps up. Sometimes, it's in front.

RUMI

I think it's what you take out of a picture that counts. There's a residue. An invisible shadow.

ANDREW WYETH

This is the only time you can study both of your shadows. If you sit perfectly still and watch your primary shadow as the sun sets you will be able to hold it long enough to see your other shadow fill up when the moon rises like a porcelain basin with clear water. If you turn carefully to face the south you may regard both of them: to understand the nature of silence you must be able to see into this space between your shadows.

BARRY LOPEZ

Drank a shadow – thought it was a snake. Got snake swallowing sickness.

CHINESE PROVERB

SILENCE

What we owe to the silence makes our ripening exact.

RAINER MARIA RILKE

A friend of mine took a Zen Buddhist monk to hear the Boston Symphony perform Beethoven's Fifth Symphony. His comment was "Not enough silence!"

WINTHROP SARGENT

Now all my teachers are dead except silence.

W.S. MERWIN

"What kind of left-overs?" asked Humkoke. "Silences," said Murke, "I collect silences." Humkoke raised his eyebrows and Murke went on. "When I have to cut tapes, in the places where the speaker sometimes pause for a moment – or sigh, or take a breath, or there is absolute silence – I don't throw that away – I collect it. I splice it together and play back the tape when I'm at home in the evening. There's not much yet, I only have three minutes so far – but then people aren't silent very often." "You know, don't you, that it's against regulations to take home sections of tape?" "Even silences?" asked Murke.

HEINRICH BÖLL

I am hoarse from silence.

THEODORE ROETHKE

Two doctors from Derby reported in 1981 about a woman, blind since the age of twenty-seven, who began to suffer deafness a few years later. "I can no longer hear the silence of lamp-posts," she said one day.

Who then tells a finer tale than any of us? Silence does.

ISAK DINESEN

The words a child speaks do not flow in a straight line, but in a curve, as if they wanted to fall back again into the silence.

MAX PICARD

This is how it always is when I finish a poem. A Great Silence overcomes me, and I wonder why I ever thought to use language.

RUMI

Not one sound fears the silence that extinguishes it.

JOHN CAGE

All the masters tell us that the reality of life – which our noisy waking consciousness prevents us from hearing – speaks to us chiefly in silence.

KARLFRIED GRAF DURCKHEIM

My propositions are elucidatory in this way: he who understands them finally recognizes them as useless... whereof one cannot speak one must be silent.

LUDWIG WITTGENSTEIN

Firelight doesn't dispel darkness; it illuminates happenings within it. Darkness remains. Darkness and silence are constant.

MCLUHAN

And as we stray further from love we multiply the words. Had we remained together we could have become a silence.

YEHUDA AMICHAI

He has occasional flashes of silence that make his conversation perfectly delightful.

SIDNEY SMITH OF THOMAS MACAULAY

Deafness isn't the opposite of hearing, it's a silence full of sounds.

MARK MEDOFF

Judicious silences are important in any work.

CLAUDE DEBUSSY

Create degrees of silence.

DON DE LILLO

How beautiful your cry that gives me your silence.

RENÉ CHAR

If silence is everywhere it is because it is about time.

DEN BOER

May my silences become more accurate.

THEODORE ROETHKE

Silence moves faster when it's going backward.

JEAN COCTEAU

SOLITUDE

There are just some things no one can do alone: conspire, be a mob, or a choir, or a regiment. Or elope.

I don't want to be anything. I want to live alone, thinking nothing, doing nothing. I want to die naturally.

TOGUCHI TUMIKO, AGE 10

A relationship in which each partner sets the other to watch over his solitude, thereby showing him the greatest confidence he has to bestow.

RAINER MARIA RILKE

The only real progress lies in learning to be wrong all alone.

ALBERT CAMUS

Solitude, my mother, tell me my life again.

O.V. DE MILOSZ

You can't be lonely on the sea – you're too alone.

TANIA AEBI

I have come one step away from everything. And here I stay, far from everything, one step away.

ANTONIO PORCHIA

What is necessary, after all, is only this: solitude, vast inner solitude. To walk inside yourself and meet no one for hours – that is what you must be able to attain.

RAINER MARIA RILKE

The man who is unable to people his solitude is also unable to be alone in a busy crowd.

CHARLES BAUDELAIRE

Just remember, we're all in this alone.

LILY TOMLIN

She knew that she had been lonely as soon as her loneliness came to an end. The birth of love is always accompanied by the idea of solitude.

PRINCESS BIBESCO

How could I be anything but a dissenter? Who wants the opinion of a group?

SAUL BELLOW

I owe my solitude to other people.

ALAN WATTS

My passionate interest in social justice and social responsibility has always stood in curious contrast to a marked lack of desire for direct association with men and women. I am a horse for single harness, not cut out for tandem or teamwork. I have never belonged wholeheartedly to country or state, to my circle of friends, or even to my family. These ties have always been accompanied by a vague aloofness and the wish to withdraw into myself increases with the years. Such isolation is bitter, but I do not regret being cut off from the understanding and sympathy of other men. I lose something by it to be sure, but I am compensated for it in being rendered independent of the customs, opinions and prejudices of others, and am not tempted to rest my peace of mind upon such shifting foundations.

ALBERT EINSTEIN

For when someone creative has found himself, he will remain in his solitude; he wants to die where he is at home.

RAINER MARIA RILKE

Without duties, almost without external communication, unconfined solitude which takes every day like a life, a spaciousness which puts no limit to vision and in the midst of which infinities surround.

RAINER MARIA RILKE

At my side only distances.

ANTONIO PORCHIA

It is the night of the ocean, the third solitude, a quivering which opens doors and wings.

PABLO NERUDA

Make your ego porous. Will is of little importance, complaining is nothing, fame is nothing. Openness, patience, receptivity, solitude is everything.

RAINER MARIA RILKE

Solitaire, precisely... I'm a realist.

JEAN RENOIR

SPECIALIZATION

I find it surprising that society thinks of specialization as logical, necessary, desirable, if not inevitable. I observe that when nature wants to make a specialist she's very good at it, whereas she seems to have designed man to be a very generally adaptable creature — by far the most adaptable creature we know of. If nature had wanted man to be a specialist, I am sure she would have grown him with one eye and a microscope on it.

BUCKMINSTER FULLER

It is a curious fact that major new steps in evolution weren't usually taken by the most advanced members of a class of animals, but by one of the more primitive and simple members of the class. The explanation for this seeming paradox is clear at once if the word "primitive" is taken to mean unspecialized, not committed to narrow behavior patterns, and if "advanced" is taken to mean specialized and locked into these patterns.

SUSUMU OHNO

Aesthetics does not exist. It seems to me that aesthetics doesn't exist as a punishment for the way it lies, pardons, panders, condescends. For the way, while knowing nothing about man, it spins its gossip about specialist subjects. Portraitists, landscapists, genre painter, still-life painter? Symbolist, acmeist, futurist? What murderous Jargon!

BORIS PASTERNAK

What we need is more people who specialize in the impossible.

THEODORE ROETHKE

Specialization is for insects.

ROBERT HEINLEIN

STARS

We literally are stardust.

JOHN HITCHCOCK, PHYSICIST

The stars sew with too fine a thread.

EUGENIO MONTALE

Of course there is nothing the matter with the stars. It is my emptiness among them while they drift farther away in the invisible morning.

W.S. MERWIN

Because of you, I again seek out the signs that precipitate desires: shooting stars, falling objects.

PABLO NERUDA

The stars come up spinning every night, bewildered in love. They'd grow tired with the revolving, if they weren't. They'd say, "How long do we have to do this!"

RUMI

But after a few minutes I sighed with relief. She didn't want the moon after all, just a tiny star, almost invisible, a little off to the side. I went to look for it.

MURILO RUBIAO

He found an enormous old umbrella in the trunk... the bright satin material had been eaten away by the moths. "Look what's left of our circus clown's umbrella," said the Colonel with one of his old phrases. Above his head a mysterious system of little metal rods opened. "The only thing it is good for now is to count the stars."

GABRIEL GARCIA MARQUEZ

Consideration (a nice word meaning putting two stars together)

BUCKMINSTER FULLER

A Prince had once told the Princess the moon was a white pearl caught in a fishnet of stars, or that it was a slice of melon eaten away by the souls of the dead. "Make up your mind," she told him, "I happen to know it is a cabbage."

Take him and cut him out in little stars, and he will make the face of heaven so fine that all the world will be in love with night.

W.B. YEATS

Note on a page with a hole burned through it: I saved this star for you but it got away.

DAVE MASON

I looked down and traced with my foot in the dust and thought again and said, "OK – any star"

WILLIAM STAFFORD

I said I will ask the stars why are you falling and they answered which of us.

W.S. MERWIN

At a dinner given by Mr. Aubert in the year 1786, William Hershel was seated next to Mr. Cavendish, the celebrated physicist, who was reputed to be the most taciturn of men. Some time passed without his uttering a word, then he suddenly turned to his neighbor and said: "I am told that you see the stars round, Dr. Herschel." "Round as a button," was the reply. A long silence ensued till, towards the end of the dinner, Cavendish again opened his lips to say in a doubtful voice: "Round as a button?" "Exactly, round as a button," repeated Herschel, and so the conversation ended.

Over and over a star became a tear. If no two are alike then what are we doing with these diagrams of loss.

ADRIENNE RICH

STARTING OVER

Degas was an incorrigible retoucher. He complained that an oil painting is never finished, and in one instance took back a pastel from a buyer, Henri Rouart, and ruined it with revision. Rouart, the story went about Paris, chained to the wall for safekeeping the painting that Degas supplied in restitution.

JOHN UPDIKE

To attempt achievement is to come back to one's starting point.

COLETTE

It doesn't, in our contemporary world, so much matter where you begin the examination of a subject, so long as you keep on till you get round again to your starting point.

EZRA POUND

Set out from any point. They are all alike. They all lead to a point of departure.

ANTONIO PORCHIA

Out of such abysses, also out of the abyss of great suspicion, one returns newborn, having shed ones skin, more ticklish and sarcastic, with a more delicate taste for joy; with a more tender tongue for all good things, with gayer senses, with a second dangerous innocence in joy, more childlike and yet a hundred times more subtle than one has ever seen before.

FRIEDRICH NIETZSCHE

And I recall an account of Trollope going up to London to pick up a rejected manuscript from a publisher, getting on the train to return home, laying the bulky bundle on his lap face down, and beginning a new book on the back pages of the rejected one.

Tennessee Williams worked every morning on whatever was at hand. If there was no play to be finished or new dialogue to be sent round to the theatre, he would open a drawer and take out the draft of a story already written and begin to rewrite it. I once found him revising a short story that had just been published. "Why," I asked, "rewrite what's already in print?" He looked at me, vaguely; then said, "Well, obviously it's not finished." And went back to his typing.

STRESS/ANXIETY

The being we do not know is an infinite being; he may arrive, and turn our anguish and our burden to dawn in our arteries.

RENÉ CHAR

Every toy has the right to break.

ANTONIO PORCHIA

Controlled hysteria is what's required. To exist constantly in a state of controlled hysteria. It's agony. But everyone has agony. The difference is that I try to take my agony home and teach it to sing.

ARTHUR MILLER

Your ship will not sink, until you put the last sixteen pound stone on it. That last stone is the piercing star that comes up at night and makes you act.

RUMI

We're like the bird which loosens a snare and then ties it tighter again in order to perfect its skill. It deprives itself of open country; it leaves behind the meadowland, while its life is spent dealing with knots.

RUMI

And windows listen for announcements of broken glass.

When faced with a crisis, put a little spittle on each earlobe and exhale deeply through the nose. Then break a chopstick. All nervousness will disappear instantly. This is a secret matter.

SEVENTEENTH-CENTURY SAMURAI MANUAL

Your plan remained the same: leave the explanation to the end or leave it out altogether. Still, you could not help but hear, each night, the muffled thud of your heart, and of hers, and the sound … of teeth.

LAWRENCE RAAB

You sit here for days saying, this is a strange business. You're the strange business. You have the energy of the sun in you, but you keep knotting it up at the base of your spine.

RUMI

I clutch at straws but what good's a brick to a drowning man?

TOM STOPPARD

STYLE

"Down with style!" Picasso had proclaimed to Malraux. "Does God have style? He made the guitar, the harlequin, the dachshund, the cat, the owl, the dove. The elephant and the whale, fine, – but the elephant and the squirrel? A real hodgepodge!

Good style is the record of powerful emotion reaching the surface of the page through fine conscious nets of restraint, caution, tact, elegance, taste, even inhibition – if the inhibition is not without honor.

ARTHUR QUILLER-COUCH

For some people, style is a very complicated way of saying very simple things; for others, it is a very simple way of saying very complicated things.

JEAN COCTEAU

SUFFERING

What's this? All that suffering for nothing, simply for a cloud?

EURIPIDES

Who has not sat before his own heart's curtain? It lifts: and the scenery is falling apart.

RAINER MARIA RILKE

You suffer captivity, but you will have furnished a word to the poem.

JORGE LUIS BORGES

And yet his grief is a great guide through this world. Even, perhaps, the surest of guides. As long as guides are needed.

W.S. MERWIN

Why the rope then, if air's so simple?

When you can't tell the difference between your own pleasure and your pain then you're an addict.

MARGARET ATWOOD

Your suffering's taste comes forth in you. Then you will love almost instantly what's tasted. No one will ever talk you out of it.

RAINER MARIA RILKE

You long to be bandaged before you have been cut.

My final belief is suffering. And I begin to believe that I do not suffer.

ANTONIO PORCHIA

Whoever finds love beneath hurt and grief disappears into emptiness with a thousand new disguises.

RUMI

You grope, delicately, breathlessly, not for the scar, but for the bandage.

W.S. MERWIN

You wound and you will wound again. Because you wound and then you go away. You do not stay with the wound.

ANTONIO PORCHIA

I do not believe in pity. What torments me tonight is the gardener's point of view.

ANTOINE DE SAINT-EXUPERY

Learn to reach deeper into the sorrows to come — to touch the almost imaginary bones under the face, to hear under the laughter the wind crying across the black stones. Kiss the mouth which tells you here, here is the world. This mouth. This laughter. These temple bones.

GALWAY KINNELL

I have no loved one, no house, no place to lead a life. All the things to which I give myself grow rich and spend me.

RAINER MARIA RILKE

It was the Buddhists who eventually made me realize that if you are waiting for a spot to hurt, it will do its best to hurt you.

SIMON

Carrying a medicine for which no one has found the disease and hoping I would make it in time.

RICHARD SHELTON

I believe that there are more urgent and honorable occupations than that incomparable waste of time we call suffering.

COLETTE

SURRENDER

But look at it my way. Here was a new geography, a mind where anything that grows grows by a kind of tour de force requiring only unconditional surrender. Here was the pure perfection of an art. Nothing like it in the British Museum.

KENNETH HANSON

That's how it goes, my friend. The problem is not falling captive, it's how to avoid surrender.

NASIM HIKMET

For when you see that the universe cannot be distinguished from how you act upon it, there is neither fate nor free will, self nor other. There is simply one all-inclusive Happening, in which your personal sensation of being alive occurs in just the same way as the river flowing and the stars shining far out in space. There is no question of submitting or accepting or going with it, for what happens in and as you is no different from what happens as it.

ALAN WATTS

I am seeing so far tonight that I am blinded by the space between me and the inevitable.

HAZEL HALL

Stop hunting. Step on this net.

RUMI

Every morning I tell myself, you can do nothing about it: submit.

JEAN COCTEAU

TEARS

My tears are full of eyes.

E.E. CUMMINGS

Somewhere an eye is filling with tears so slowly it takes hours.

DAVID P. YOUNG

You do not see the river of mourning because it lacks one tear of your own.

ANTONIO PORCHIA

I still have the little handkerchief that was saturated with your tears; I carry it on me as a symbol that, on my heart, all your tears will be dried, always, friend, all your tears.

RAINER MARIA RILKE

Time to plant tears, says the Almanac.

ELIZABETH BISHOP

Count me back to your mercy with the measures of a bitter song, and do not separate me from my tears.

LEONARD COHEN

There is a palace that opens only to tears.

ZOHAR

Tears of the candles. Veins full of feathers.

W.S. MERWIN

Tears of eyes. Unhappiness of the unhappy. Unhappiness without interest and tears without color.

PAUL ELUARD

How have you come to be so thin. Why are you trembling. Why are you so pale, oh simple girl, and she answered the lord of her life, all these things just happen for no reason sighing as she said it and turning to let tears fall.

500 BC - 1000 AD CLASSICAL SANSKRIT

You're crying. You say you've burned yourself. But can you think of anyone who's not hazy with smoke?

RUMI

TENDERNESS/GENTLENESS

Tenderness contains an element of sadness. It is not the sadness of feeling sorry for yourself or feeling deprived but it is a natural situation of fullness. You feel so full and rich, as if you were about to shed tears. Your eyes are full of tears, and the moment you blink, the tears will spill out of your eyes and roll down your cheeks. In order to be a good warrior, one has to feel this sad and tender heart.

CHOGYAM TRUNGPA

O gently, gently… Do something for him, – take him close to the garden, give him the full weight of night… preserve him.

RAINER MARIA RILKE

Then, violence is a clumsy tool and an unusable one, and that is why the spirit always lags behind it, the spirit which knows nothing of force, whose conquests are won by the power of invincible gentleness.

RAINER MARIA RILKE

Koichi Tsujimura defines the 'holy fool' of Zen as a "man capable in every simple and daily thing, of seeing the One and letting it act. Such a capacity is gentleness, gratitude, and mercy toward each thing, not only toward men, but toward everything that exists."

TSUJIMURA

A poem writes itself out: its title – the dream of all poems and the text of all lovers – "Tenderness toward existence."

GALWAY KINNELL

THINKING

Thinking: freeing birds, erasing images, burying lamps.

PABLO NERUDA

The highest form of operational thinking: the ability to hypothetically consider any state along a continuum of possibility as potentially equal to any other state, and return to the same state from which the operation began.

JEAN PIAGET

"What would you say is your biggest handicap?" she said. "Thinking," he said. "I'm always thinking about thinking, and not doing much real thinking."

EDNA O'BRIEN

John Dewey was nearer the mark when he described thought as "active uncertainty."

It is a profoundly erroneous truism, repeated by all the copy books, and by eminent people when they are making speeches, that we should cultivate the habit of thinking what we are doing. The precise opposite is the case.

ALFRED NORTH WHITEHEAD

Our heads are round so that our thoughts can fly in any direction.

FRANCIS PICABIA

Most people would die sooner than think; in fact, they do so.

BERTRAND RUSSELL

When my body thinks... all my flesh has a soul.

COLETTE

Story by Jung of a conversation with a chief of the Pueblo Indians: Jung asked the chief's opinion of the white man and was told that it was not a high one. White people, said Ochwiay Biano, seem always upset, always restlessly looking for something, with the result that their faces are covered with wrinkles. He added that white men must be crazy because they think with their heads, and it is well known that only crazy people do that. Jung asked in surprise how the Indian thought, to which Ochwiay Biano replied that naturally he thought with his heart.

LAURENS VAN DER POST

Don't think: Look.

LUDWIG WITTGENSTEIN

Tolstoy and his brother, when they were boys, formed a club, initiation into which required that the candidate stand in a corner for half-an-hour and not think of a white bear.

THIRD ALTERNATIVE

There's an alternative. There's always a third way, and it's not a combination of the other two ways. It's a different way.

DAVID CARRADINE

Between living and dreaming is a third thing. Guess it.

TIME

We are trying to say there is still time but we know it is only now in a different costume and it is too late.

RICHARD SHELTON

Time is merely a device to keep everything from happening at once.

In a journal entry for January 8, 1966, Joseph Cornell asserted that he lived one day ahead of conventional time.

Time is not a road – it is a room.

JOHN FOWLES

The saddest thing, mister, is a watch: 11, 12, 1, 2....

It is getting urgent by the minute not to erase the clock but to drop the way we use it.

JOHN CAGE

In the late seventeenth century, M. de Villayer designed a clock so arranged that when he reached for the hour hand at night, it guided him to a small container with a spice inserted in place of numbers, a different spice for each hour of the night. Even when he could not see the clock, he could always taste the time.

DANIEL BOORSTIN

BREATHING ON YOUR OWN

Recently, a group of Midwestern farmers who opposed the introduction of Daylight Saving Time in their region summarized their position by pointing out that "the extra hour of sunlight will burn the grass."

And even down there time continues, waiting, raining on the dust, eager to erase even absence.

PABLO NERUDA

God has infinite time to give us; but how did he give it? In one immense tract of lazy millenniums? No. He cut it up into a neat succession of new mornings.

RALPH WALDO EMERSON

Ts'ui Pen did not think of time as absolute and uniform. He believed in an infinite series of times, in a dizzily growing ever spreading network of diverging, converging and parallel times. This web of time – the strands of which approach one another, bifurcate, intersect, or ignore each other through centuries – embraces every possibility. We do not exist in most of them. In some you exist and not I, while in others I do and you do not, and in yet others both of us exist. In this one, in which chance has favored me, you have come to my gate. In another you, crossing the garden, have found me dead. In yet another, I say these very same words, but am an error, a phantom.

JORGE LUIS BORGES

Time is a great teacher, but unfortunately it kills all its pupils.

HECTOR BERLIOZ

Tell me what you think of time, and I'll tell you what I think of you.

DR. HUMPHREY OSMOND

He pointed out, too, how difficult it would be to break off the engagement at the eleventh hour. "But that's just the beauty of the eleventh hour. That's what it's there for, surely," he said.

MAURICE BARING

I feel very comfortable talking in nanoseconds. I sit at one of these analyzers and nanoseconds are wide. I mean you can see them go by. Jesus, I say, that signal takes twelve nanoseconds to get from there to there. Those are real big things to me when I'm building a computer. Yet, when I think about it, how much longer it takes to snap your fingers, I've lost touch of what a nanosecond really means. (The snap of a finger is equivalent to the passage of 500 million nanoseconds.)

TRACY KIDDER

TRANSLATION

(Computer as translator of human language) The senator was asked to produce an English phrase for translation and promptly suggested, "Out of sight, out of mind." The machine dutifully whirred and winked and generated a piece of paper on which were printed a few Chinese characters. But the senator could not read Chinese. So, to complete the test, the program was run in reverse, the Chinese characters input and an English output. The visitors crowded around the new piece of paper, which to their initial puzzlement read: "Invisible idiot."

CARL SAGAN

British: "I know it like the back of my hand." Russian: "I know it like the palm of my hand." American: " … inside out." German: "like the inside of my pocket." Spaniard: "as if I'd given birth to it." Thailander: "like a snake swimming in water."

The slogan "Come Alive With Pepsi" was translated in China as: "Pepsi Brings Your Ancestors Back From The Grave."

In English dogs bark "bow wow" or "arf arf". But in German, dogs go "wau wau", in Chinese, "wang wang", in Vietnamese "gau gau" and in Japanese, "wan wan". In Yiddish, dogs go "how how".

TRUTH/LIES

We all know that Art is not truth. Art is a lie that makes us realize truth, at least the truth that is given us to understand. The artist must know the manner whereby to convince others of the truthfulness of his lies.

PABLO PICASSO

People need good lies. There are too many bad ones.

KURT VONNEGUT JR.

The greatest enemy of any one of our truths may be the rest of our truths.

WILLIAM JAMES

I am a lie that always tells the truth.

JEAN COCTEAU

Happiness is being able to speak the truth without hurting anyone.

FEDERICO FELLINI

Truth is in all things, even partly, in error.

JEAN-LUC GODARD

One must use a brazen lie to convince people of a reality of a higher and deeper order.

JEAN COCTEAU

How many there are who, weary of lying, commit suicide in any truth at all.

ANTONIO PORCHIA

Where did the truth go? The key was mislaid in an army of doors, it was there on its ring with the others, but the lock is nowhere in the world. No world for the key to get lost in, no true or false, in the end.

PABLO NERUDA

Those who try to tell the truth are spies without passwords, smuggling bits of silence past the sentries.

There might actually occur a case where we should say, "This man believes he is pretending."

LUDWIG WITTGENSTEIN

Do not believe the truth. The truth is tiny compared to what you have to do.

LEONARD COHEN

The experience is there, the reality is there, but how to get at it? Everything I type turns into a lie simply because it is not the truth.

JOYCE CAROL OATES

He tried to sing, singing not to remember his true life of lies and to remember his lying life of truths.

OCTAVIO PAZ

Sometimes, surely, truth is closer to imagination – or to intelligence, to love – than to fact? To be accurate is not to be right.

SHIRLEY HAZZARD

Frank Harris told the truth, according to Max Beerbohm, only "when his invention flagged."

VINCENT BROME

Listeners, I have come far to keep it from making a difference whether I lie or tell the truth.

WILLIAM STAFFORD

I do not mind lying, but I hate inaccuracy.

SAMUEL BUTLER

Truth is a great flirt.

FRANZ LISZT

I had always liked the story about Johnny Kerr, the pro basket-ball player with bad legs who set a record for consecutive games. Clearly, he played in pain. After he had set the record, he was asked how he could play hurt night after night. His answer: "I tell my legs lies."

In order for a proposition to be capable of being true, it must also be capable of being false.

LUDWIG WITTGENSTEIN

The difference between the truth and a lie weighs no more than a feather.

EGYPTIAN SAYING

If one tells the truth, one is sure, sooner or later, to be found out.

OSCAR WILDE

For example is no proof.

YIDDISH PROVERB

One of the favorite maxims of my father was the distinction between the two sorts of truths, profound truths recognized by the fact that the opposite is also a profound truth, in contrast to trivialities where opposites are obviously absurd.

HANS BOHR OF HIS FATHER NEILS BOHR

In order to reach the truth, it is necessary, once in one's life, to put everything in doubt – so far as possible.

DESCARTES

If you want to be true to life, start lying about it.

JOHN FOWLES

Truth only reveals itself when one gives up all preconceived ideas.

SHOSEKI

The metaphysicians of Tilon are not looking for truth, not even an approximation of it; they are after a kind of amazement.

JORGE LUIS BORGES

A little inaccuracy sometimes saves tons of explanation.

H.H. MUNRO (SAKI)

To see truth, contemplate all phenomena as a lie.

THAGAMAPA

One of the great lessons he'd learned in poetry, James Dickey said, was from Monroe Spears who taught him at Vanderbilt in the nineteen-forties. Spears had been telling him what he needed to do to improve a particular poem. Dickey had said "It didn't happen that way." And Spears had told him "No artist is bound by the truth."

James Dickey had always been interested in "the creative possibilities of the lie." He believe that the poet "is not trying to tell the truth, but to make it."

The truth, he thought, has never been of any real value to any human being – it is a symbol for mathematicians and philosophers to pursue. In human relations kindness and lies are worth a thousand truths.

GRAHAM GREENE

The truth is at the bottom of a well. You look in a well and you see the sun or the moon, but if you jump in there's no longer the sun or the moon, there's the truth.

SCIASCIA

Whether it happened so or not I do not know; but if you think about it you can see that it is true.

BLACK ELK

Everything one invents is true, you may be perfectly sure of that. Poetry is as precise as geometry.

GUSTAVE FLAUBERT

I want my paintings to be anomalous in such a way that they become lies, if you like, but lies that are more truthful than the literal truth.

VAN GOGH

At a certain point all stories are true.

JAMES SALTER

Truth is completely spontaneous. Lies have to be taught.

BUCKMINSTER FULLER

UNION OF OPPOSITES

I happen to feel that the degree of a person's intelligence is directly reflected by the number of conflicting attitudes she can bring to bear on the same topic.

LISA ALTHER

Unfortunately, our Western mind, lacking all culture in this respect, has never yet devised a concept, nor even a name, for the union of opposites through the middle path, that most fundamental item of inner experience, which could respectably be set against the Chinese concept of Tao.

CARL JUNG

Between yea and nay, how much difference is there?

LAO TZU

I thought finally that of all the nostalgias that haunt the human heart the greatest of them all, for me, is an everlasting longing to bring what is youngest home to what is oldest, in us all.

LAURENS VAN DER POST

The light that puts out our eyes is darkness to us.

HENRY DAVID THOREAU

That which is one is one. That which is not one, is also one.

CHIANG TZU

Everything leads me to believe that there is a certain point in the life of the spirit at which life and death, the real and the imagined, the past and the future, the communicable and the incommunicable, the exalted and the lowly, cease to be seen as contradictory.

Light is half a companion.

GENOESE PROVERB

Roots and wings. But let the wings grow roots and the roots fly.

JUAN RAMON JIMENEZ

By being both here and beyond I am becoming a horizon.

Everything that happens is at once natural and inconceivable.

E.M. CIORAN

Nothing is far away. Everything is near.

CHANDIDAS

We were parted (long) ago, yet we have not been separated even for a moment. We are facing each other all day long, yet we have never met.

D.T. SUZUKI

Albert Rothenberg put this type of creative insight strategy simply: It is "the creator's ability to actively conceive of multiple opposites or antitheses simultaneously."

A singing between the chance and the requirement.

PABLO NERUDA

Everything is a little bit of darkness, even the light.

ANTONIO PORCHIA

He who being a man, remains a woman, will become a universal channel.

LAO-TZU

I've heard it said there's a window that opens from one mind to another, but if there is no wall, there is no need for fitting the window or the latch.

RUMI

UNIVERSE

One must give back the stare of the universe. Anybody can.

HORTENSE CALISHER

Using the mathematics that, as we have seen, provide physicists with their uncanny power of analysis, Hugh Everett III came to the conclusion that "we live in an infinite number of continually interacting universes." Moreover, in this system of an infinite number of parallel universes "all possible futures really happen."

We see the universe the way it is because if it were different, we would not be here to observe it.

STEPHEN HAWKING

In a single, unfurnished room of the hotel, Salvador Dali kept a large, beautiful helium balloon that he visited at various times during the day, noting and delighting in its autonomous, barely perceptible movements. "I am penetrating more and more into the compressed magic of the universe." Dali said.

I'm looking for the face I had before the world was made.

W.B. YEATS

There is another world, but it is in this one.

PAUL ELUARD

If you wish to make an apple pie from scratch, you must first create the universe.

CARL SAGAN

You know, it's just like I understood the universe but I can't find my mailbox.

WELDON BUTLER

WHOLE/FRAGMENTS

This is not a time in which to complete anything. It is a time for fragments.

MARCEL DUCHAMP

We all have reasons for moving. I move to keep thing whole.

MARK STRAND

In this story, the boy Chi Po is taking painting lessons from the sorcerer, Bu Fu. At one point, Bu Fu is looking at Chi Po's painting and says: "No, no. You have merely painted what is. Anybody can paint what is! The real secret is to paint what isn't." Upon which Chi Po was very puzzled and said, "But what is there that isn't?"

OSCAR MANDEL

Break your pitcher against a rock. We don't need any longer to haul pieces of the Ocean around.

RUMI

I hold a great deal against this system of organization, that is (the separation of things which should not be separated). We categorize everyone. We send the old here, the young there: We ship adolescents off to war. We send everyone to prison every day: the children to school, the parents to the office or the factory, the musicians to concert halls in the evening.

JOHN CAGE

The breaking of a wave cannot explain the whole sea.

VLADIMIR NABOKOV

You cannot stir things apart.

TOM STOPPARD

WONDER

My own habitual feeling is that the world is so extremely odd, and everything in it so surprising. Why should there be green grass and liquid water, and why have I got hands and feet?

DON JOHN CHAPMAN

Now my own suspicion is that the universe is not only queerer than we suppose, but queerer than we can suppose.

J.B.S. HALDANE

How could I have expected that after a long life I would understand no more than to wake up at night and to repeat: strange, strange, strange, O how strange, how strange, O how funny and strange.

CZESLAW MILOSZ

Picasso insisted that everything was miraculous — it was miraculous he said, that one did not melt in one's bath.

The nineteenth-century physicist Michael Faraday said: "Nothing is too wonderful to be true."

BREATHING ON YOUR OWN

They say that every snowflake is different. If that were true, how could the world go on? How could we ever get up off our knees? How could we ever recover from the wonder of it?

JEANETTE WINTERSON

At the moment you are most in awe of all there is about life that you don't understand, you are closer to understanding it all than at any other time.

JANE WAGNER

So, when all is said and done, I think Derek Walcott was right: One has to be willing to surrender to a condition of awe, to the astonishment of the soul, to bewilderment, bafflement, humility. Or, as Emerson neatly put it, "Let the bird sing without deciphering the song."

DENNIS SHEKERJIAN

It is to a poet a thing of awe to find that his story is true.

ISAK DINESEN

I am so small I can barely be seen. How can this great love be inside me? Look at your eyes. They are small, but they see enormous things.

RUMI

The world will not perish for want of wonders, but for want of wonder.

J.B.S. HALDANE

I am glad that my Master lived in a one-story house when I began to traverse the early stages of love. For when he would speak of the wonders and the beauty of creation, I could not control my happiness and would commence a dance that most always resulted in – a dive, head first, out of his window. And you only broke your big nose seventeen times.

HAFIZ

The whole order of things is as outrageous as any miracle which could presume to violate it.

G.K. CHESTERTON

Everything is a miracle. We just have to recognize it.

FEDERICO FELLINI

WRITING

Learning words have the blood of birds.

PAUL CARROLL

Once, my sister, glancing out of a window, saw Wallace Stevens going by her house. As she watched, he slowed down, came to a stop, rocked in place for a moment or two, took a step backward, hesitated, then strode confidently forward – left, right, left, right – on his way to work. It was obvious to her that Stevens had gone back over a phrase, dropped an unsatisfactory word, inserted a superior one, and proceeded to the next line of the poem he was making.

BRENDAN GILL

Beside these general and, unfortunately, unreliable methods, a number of creative persons have stumbled upon a variety of specific ways to enhance their own powers. Most of these, however are purely idiosyncratic, and of no help to the rest of us. Schiller wrote best when smelling rotting apples; Zola was stimulated by the ambience of artificial light, even at midday; the naturalist Comte de Buffon felt inspired only when dressed as if for a social event. Ben Jonson responded to the influences of tea, the purring of a cat, and the odor of orange peel, and Andre Gretry composed with his feet in ice water. Einstein and Freud both worked particularly well during bouts of abdominal discomfort (though neither deliberately induced such distress as an aid to creativity.)

BREATHING ON YOUR OWN

You know, she said, I've read your last story, and I ought to have
returned it weeks ago. It isn't right. It's almost right. It almost
works. But not quite. You are too literary. You must not be literary. Suppress all the literature and it will work.

COLETTE TO GEORGES SIMENON

If only there were a perfect word I could give to you – a word like
some artichoke that could sit on the table, dry, and become itself.

SANDRA HOCHMAN

The problem is not whether the song will continue, but whether
a dark space can be found where the notes can resonate.

RAINER MARIA RILKE

But to say what you want to say, You must create another language
and nourish it for years and years with what you have loved, with
what you have lost, with what you will never find again.

GEORGE SEFERIS

From his earliest infancy he was remarkable for his great fond-
ness for reading, so that when any of his family went to distant
markets or fairs, he constantly importuned them to bring him
presents of books; which, if they returned home later than his
usual hour of going to rest, were always taken up to bed to him;
and sometimes when they had been forgotten, his mother had
no other means to allure him to sleep but by wrapping a piece
of wood in paper like a book, which he would then hug to his
pillow till the morning discovered the deception.

TREADWAY RUSSELL NASH OF WILLIAM SHENSTONE

When I stop drinking tea and eating bread and butter I say, "I've
had enough." But when I stop reading poems or novels I say,
"No more of that, no more of that."

ANTON CHEKHOV

Now I live only in the company of a few disobedient words.

KARL KROLOW

212

BREATHING ON YOUR OWN

Some years ago a young scholar who greatly admired A.E. Houseman's work wrote to the poet and asked him how he managed always to select the right word. Houseman replied that he didn't bother about trying to get the right word, he simply bothered about getting rid of the wrong one.

And all the time it's your own story, even when you think — "It's all just made up, a trick. What is the author trying to do?" Reader, we are in such a story: All of this is trying to arrange a kind of prayer for you. Pray for me.

WILLIAM STAFFORD

All good writing is swimming under water and holding your breath.

F. SCOTT FITZGERALD

Paul would take from his pockets his notebook, his fountain pen and a little packet of cardboard cards. "What are you doing, Paul?" "I'm working. I'm working at my job. I'm employed by the Library Catalogue for the Nationale, I'm noting down titles." "Uh ... can you do that from memory?" "From memory? What good is that? I'm doing better than that. I've noticed that the Nationale is very poor in Latin and Italian works of the fifteenth century.... So until the day when these lacunae are remedied by luck or scholarship, I'm making notes of highly interesting works that should have been written... so at least the titles will maintain the Catalogue's prestige." "But," said I naively, "you mean the books have never been written?" "Ah," he replied with an offhand shrug, "I can't be expected to do everything."

COLETTE AND PAUL MASSON

If you have any sense you write the kind of novel other people write, but the trick is you can't write the sort of novel anyone else has already written.

JAMES CAIN

What can be said, lacks reality. Only what fails to make its way into words exists and counts.

E.M. CIORAN

Letters frighten me more than anything else in life. They contain greater possibilities of murder than any poison. I think you ought only to write to a person when you are in the same place and quite certain to see them. When a letter is a continuation of presence it is all right, but when it becomes a codification of absence it is intolerable. Please write to me.

ELIZABETH BIBESCO

According to Paley, the Bishop was once impatient at the slowness of his Carlisle printer. "Why does not my book make its appearance?" he said to the printer. "My Lord, I am extremely sorry, but we have been obliged to send to Glasgow for a pound of parentheses."

BOSWELL, OF DR. EDMUND LOW

I know I was writing stories when I was five. I don't know what I did before that. Just loafed I suppose.

P.G. WODEHOUSE

It is what is left over when everything explainable has been explained that makes a story worth writing and reading.

FLANNERY O'CONNOR

An author who claims to write for posterity must be a bad one. We should never know for whom we write.

E.M. CIORAN

He kept, as it were, a harem of words, to which he was constant and absolutely faithful. Some he favored more than others, but he neglected none. He used them more often out of compliment than of necessity.

ALICE MEYNELL, OF SWINBURNE

I never quite know when I'm not writing. Sometimes my wife comes up to me at a party and says, "Dammit, Thurber, stop writing." She usually catches me in the middle of a paragraph.

JAMES THURBER

BREATHING ON YOUR OWN

During his years of poverty Balzac lived in an unheated and almost unfurnished garret. On one of the bare walls the writer inscribed the words: "Rosewood paneling with commode"; on another: "Gobelin tapestry with Venetian mirror." and in the place of honor over the empty fireplace: "Picture by Raphael."

E. FULLER

I suppose most editors are failed writers – but so are most writers.

T.S. ELIOT

Remarks are not literature.

GERTRUDE STEIN

It is what you read when you don't have to that determines what you will be when you can't help it.

OSCAR WILDE

This is the time for what can be said. Here is its country. Speak and testify.

RAINER MARIA RILKE

When I used to teach creative writing, I would tell the students to make their characters want something right away – even if it's only a glass of water. Characters paralyzed by the meaninglessness of modern life still have to drink water from time to time.

KURT VONNEGUT, JR.

Writing is very easy; all you do is sit staring at a blank sheet of paper until the drops of blood form on your forehead.

GENE FOWLER

If I had to give young writers advice, I'd say don't listen to writers talking about writing.

LILLIAN HELLMAN

We write to taste life twice.

ANAIS NIN

Writing a novel is like driving a car at night. You can see only as far as your headlights, but you can make the whole trip that way.

E. L. DOCTOROW

The whole secret of writing, as Wodehouse said, is applying the seat of the trousers to the seat of the chair.

H. N. Swanson was a book agent who represented Raymond Chandler. When he was asked what kind of writing was the most profitable, Swanson replied "ransom notes."

Once I planned to write a book of poems entirely about the things in my pocket. But I found it would be too long: and the age of the great epics is past.

G.K. CHESTERTON

I read the newspaper avidly. It is my one form of continuous fiction.

ANEURIN BEVAN

He seemed at once preoccupied, knowledgeable, worldly, remote, detached, vain, skeptical, eccentric, self-sufficient, indestructible, egomaniacal, and hospitable to praise. He was like almost every other writer I had known in my life.

PAUL THEROUX

If you are in difficulties with a book, try the element of surprise; attack it at an hour when it isn't expecting it.

H. G. WELLS

Or he mentions the village librarian, constrained by a small budget, who reads the reviews of books and then, conscientiously, himself writes the books for his library shelves.

BEREL LANG ABOUT JORGE LUIS BORGES

Language is fossil poetry.

RALPH WALDO EMERSON

Writers should "occupy themselves only with their own mean-ingless, innocent intoxications."

VLADIMIR NABOKOV

They ask me if I were on a desert island and knew nobody would ever see what I wrote, would I go on writing. My answer is most emphatically yes, I would go on writing for company.

WILLIAM BURROUGHS

ZERO

When you get there, there isn't any there there.

GERTRUDE STEIN

There is no out there out there.

JOHN WHEELER

The problem is; to get back to zero.

JEAN-LUC GODARD